SURVIVING SOLO
MOTHERHOOD

WELBECK
BALANCE

ABOUT THE AUTHORS

Journalist Amy Rose suddenly became a single mother during Christmas 2018, turning her life upside down. She documents her solo parenting – and mental health – journey on Instagram (@by.amyrose) and empowers other women in similar situations. Amy lives in Peterborough, UK, with son Milo and bunny Bluebell.

Dr Emma Cotterill is a clinical psychologist experienced in supporting people with a range of mental health difficulties. Alongside individual psychological therapy work, Emma is a trainer, writer and supervisor, and is passionate about mental health education and supporting wellbeing. Emma co-parents her two boys in Surrey, UK.

SURVIVING SOLO MOTHERHOOD

HOW TO LOOK AFTER YOUR MENTAL HEALTH AND BOOST YOUR EMOTIONAL WELLBEING AS A SINGLE MUM

AMY ROSE AND DR EMMA COTTERILL

WELBECK
BALANCE

Published in 2022 by Welbeck Balance
An imprint of Welbeck Trigger Ltd
Part of Welbeck Publishing Group
Based in London and Sydney.
www.welbeckpublishing.com

A CIP catalogue record for this book is available from the British Library

ISBN
Trade Paperback – 978-1-80129-011-1

Typeset by Lapiz Digital Services
Printed in Great Britain by CPI Group (UK) Ltd, Croydon CRO 4YY

10 9 8 7 6 5 4 3 2 1

Note/Disclaimer
Welbeck Balance encourages diversity and different viewpoints. However, all
views, thoughts, and opinions expressed in this book are the author's own and are
not necessarily representative of Welbeck Publishing Group as an organization.
All material in this book is set out in good faith for general guidance; Welbeck
Publishing Group makes no representations or warranties of any kind, express or
implied, with respect to the accuracy, completeness, suitability or currency of the
contents of this book, and specifically disclaims, to the extent permitted by law,
any implied warranties of merchantability or fitness for a particular purpose and
any injury, illness, damage, death, liability or loss incurred, directly or indirectly
from the use or application of any of the information contained in this book.
This book is not intended to replace expert medical or psychiatric advice. It is
intended for informational purposes only and for your own personal use and
guidance. It is not intended to diagnose, treat or act as a substitute for professional
medical advice. The author and the publisher are not medical practitioners nor
counsellors, and professional advice should be sought before embarking on any
health-related programme.

www.welbeckpublishing.com

To Amanda and Jemma, the most badass single mums
I get to call my friends. And to Milo, for spending hours
on Roblox while I type away. I love you.

Amy

To all the single mothers out there, who are doing the best
they can through this challenging journey. And to my boys
who make everything worthwhile. Love you.

Emma

CONTENTS

Introduction – Where You Are, Right Now   xi

PART ONE Feeling All the Feelings   1

1   Grief and Loss   3
2   Rage, Anger and Frustration   37
3   Shame   69
4   Guilt   86
5   Anxiety, Panic and Overwhelm   110
6   Depression   140

PART TWO Moving Forward   169

7   From Powerless to Powerful   171
8   Finding Joy   191
9   Love, Lust and Everything In Between   206
10   How to Navigate a New Relationship   232
11   Finding You – Positive Mental Health and Embracing
     Single Motherhood   252

Final Words   269

Acknowledgements   270
Useful Resources   271

INTRODUCTION

Welcome to solo motherhood. You may have been a single mother since your pregnancy, or you have found yourself divorced with nearly grown-up children. You might find yourself here because your partner has sadly passed away; or you or they were the person to leave. Perhaps you are starting this journey as a result of exiting a difficult relationship, or you are starting it joyful in the knowledge that this is the best thing for your family. Whatever your situation, this is uncharted territory that we would like to help you navigate.

WHERE YOU ARE, RIGHT NOW

You're going solo. First things first, congratulations on surviving this far; you are an absolute superhero!

Relationships are complicated – ending them, even more so. Whether you walked out the door, mutually ended the relationship, or were the one who was left behind, the end of a relationship is an emotionally draining experience – especially when children are involved.

So, you might be struggling with how on earth you are going to survive solo motherhood. How will you cope with the grief, the guilt, the shame and the sheer significance of the change in your personal situation? How will you get to a place where you are content and feel like you're bossing this solo-motherhood journey? Well, it's going to be a journey indeed; there will be ups and there will be downs. But you will get through this. And we are here to help you.

WHAT THIS BOOK AIMS TO DO

This book is your support, through whatever life is throwing at you. We aim to be your lifeline when you're not sure where to turn, the friend that knows how you're feeling, and perhaps even a wise sage offering you some really good advice.

The book explores the various emotions that come with solo motherhood, including grief, anger, shame, guilt, anxiety and depression in Part One; as well as the positive aspects that can come out of your newfound status, such as finding your power, joy, love, independence, fresh partnerships and discovering a whole new you in Part Two.

Each chapter looks at the practical and psychological impact of these emotions and experiences on you and your child/children; provides first-hand experience from a diverse range of solo mums; and shares advice and guidance on how to manage these emotions and situations to help you on your journey to surviving, and thriving, in solo motherhood.

ABOUT US

This book is a collaboration written by both of us, Amy and Dr Emma. Here's a bit about us before you step into this book:

AMY'S STORY

I'm Amy Rose, a journalist and writer. Just before Christmas 2018, my son's dad left me. I had absolutely no idea what to do with myself. I didn't know how to deal with all the emotions that came with it, and I did not realize how much this break-up would affect my mental health, and not just in the "expected" ways like heartbreak and upset. It induced rage in me; it made me feel ashamed; it made me anxious; it made me feel guilty.

And I certainly grieved for that relationship for a lot longer than I would have liked.

Eventually, I started feeling more positive, and saw how – through simple steps I incorporated into my daily life – I was growing as a person and becoming more self-assured and much more confident. Now, I'm (still) a single mum – despite another relationship, but you'll hear all about that later – and my son, Milo, is thriving.

I hope that by sharing my lived experience, alongside Dr Emma's professional guidance, this book will help to support you throughout your journey.

DR EMMA'S STORY
I'm Emma and I'm a clinical psychologist. In my work, I have supported many people going through separation, divorce and single parenting. I have supported people through the grief, loss, anxiety, depression, shame, guilt, worry and powerlessness, and also through the dating process and the experience of finding themselves and their strength and power as a single parent.

On a personal level, I am a mum to two amazing boys who I co-parent with their dad. I have experienced all the processes we talk about in the book, and hope to bring both my personal and professional experiences to the guidance and support I can offer alongside Amy's amazing, honest, real words.

We hope this book gives you the space to reflect on yourself and your journey. You've been through so much already, so taking stock and reflecting on where you are now and where you want to be is a very positive step in your journey to a happier experience of solo motherhood.

PART ONE

FEELING ALL THE FEELINGS

1

GRIEF AND LOSS

It's happened. You find yourself here: a single parent, trying to figure out how on earth to feel, to think, to cope; wondering how you will even begin to get through this new chapter of your life. As you try to make sense of the ending of your relationship and your life as a "family", and try to figure out how to move into your new life as a single parent, grief, loss and loneliness are often present, overwhelming, devastating and all-consuming.

As with any grief, grieving the loss of a relationship, a partner, a family, a future, is a process (see page 6). Grieving involves: working through all the emotions the grief and loss bring; making sense of what has happened; letting go of what you thought you knew about your future; and accepting that it was not the future for you.

> *It took me a long time to come to the realization that the family life I had planned was not meant to be. I still have moments today where I mourn the idea of the "typical" family set-up. When I was a little girl, there was no way I would have imagined becoming a single mother to a five-year-old at the age of 26. While all my friends were just starting to settle down with someone and think about starting families, I was in a very different situation: alone and with a child.* **Amy**

SURVIVING SOLO MOTHERHOOD

Experiencing grief and loss when a relationship ends is completely normal and understandable. Grief is triggered by loss, and when a relationship with a partner breaks down, with a child/family involved, there are many potential losses. These losses include not only loss of the relationship, but also loss of the family set-up, loss of a planned future, loss of support, loss of finances, loss of the social life you knew, and so much more.

Grief and loss can happen whether you wanted the relationship to end, or you didn't. They can happen whether a relationship ends suddenly or slowly reaches this conclusion over time. Grief and loss are, of course, experienced devastatingly when a partner passes away. And it can also occur when a separation happens, and you have to navigate having your ex-partner in your life constantly as a co-parent (whether amicably or not), or if you have to now figure out how to parent alone while your ex-partner has no contact (whether through your choice or theirs or due to legal decisions).

In this chapter, we're going to explore how grieving and loss following the end of a relationship looks, and share experiences from people who have been there and experienced this. We will be sharing experiences of grief ranging from a divorce after 25 years of marriage with three teenaged children, to a romantic fling that ended even before the child was born. We'll look at how each person experienced or dealt with their grief, and what positive steps we can take to manage our own grief.

GRIEF THROUGH A WIDE LENS

Please note, in this chapter we will talk about grief through a wide lens (for example, related to the many losses and related grief that people experience after a relationship breakdown involving children). We are aware that there are some devastating circumstances where the relationship ends and you find yourself a single parent because of the death of a partner. If this is your experience, it is so important to allow yourself time to grieve, to take care of yourself, and to seek help and support as you need. We hope that this chapter, and the whole of this book, provides you with a source of comfort, advice and support on your journey into solo motherhood, while also being aware that this book is not specific to the death of a partner, in and you may wish to seek specific support.

WHAT IS GRIEF?

So, what do we mean when we talk about grief? Grief is a natural and understandable response to loss; it can be an intense and powerful emotion that can bring with it sadness, anger, shock, fear, loneliness, panic and anxiety. In some circumstances there can be guilt and shame intertwined with grief, which can be very upsetting to make sense of and work through. Grief can also be very physical, leading to exhaustion and fatigue, aches and pains, loss of appetite and lack of sleep.

For Amy, grief showed up when her partner told her he didn't love her anymore and left the house. When she was grieving, the emotions she experienced were extreme sadness, anxiety and lots of fear. When she understood that grief and fear are often linked, this made perfect sense to her.

I was terrified of how I was going to cope mentally as a single parent before I even started thinking about all the practicalities and logistics. This was the fear of the unknown, and how I was going to adjust to a life I had not planned for. **Amy**

You too may experience a lot of these emotions, and more. And, of course, these emotions can exist outside of the grief process too; we will delve into these different emotions more throughout the book.

THE COMMON STAGES OF GRIEF WHEN A RELATIONSHIP ENDS

Grief is both an emotion and a process. Research has shown us that one way of understanding grief is through the five common stages to the grieving process. The Kubler-Ross model of grief (*On Death and Dying*, Macmillan, New York, 1969) described these stages as denial (shock), anger, depression, bargaining and acceptance. Below, we explain how these stages apply to the loss of a relationship. While these are five identifiable stages, the process is not linear; that is, you are unlikely to move neatly through each stage one by one. Instead, you may experience the stages in any order; you may experience some stages at the same time; you may move back and forward between stages; and you may well experience one stage more intensely than another.

Denial/Shock

To begin with you may feel shock, and be in denial about the relationship ending or being about to end, or about the reality of becoming a single mother. You may find it hard to grasp this new reality in your mind, finding it so unbearable or unbelievable that this could be happening. It may feel impossible to picture this new future, and you may hold on to the idea that this break-up can't happen, won't happen. You may feel numb, frozen, unable to comprehend. You may also experience panic and anxiety as the shock hits you.

When my ex left me, I spent around four days in bed. Thankfully, my best friend came to look after me and my son, otherwise I don't know how I would have coped. Every day on waking, I was met with a sinking feeling as I remembered that this was my life now. It felt was like I was mourning our relationship, the family that we had been building, and my life as I knew it. **Amy**

Anger

Understanding that anger is a normal part of how we process grief is important, as anger is a very common emotion in the midst of the end of a relationship.

You might be angry at the situation or events that led to your break-up. You might feel anger that the relationship is ending and that your future is changing. You might feel anger for what your child will go through, or anger toward your ex-partner for leaving or for their behaviour. You might feel anger at yourself for what has happened (this can also interlink with guilt or shame, depending on the circumstances). You might be feeling helpless and out of control which is then making you feel angry.

Your anger may spin in all kinds of ways, in all directions; it may be big and intense, or a low simmering frustration or irritation.

Anger, of course, when not supported well, can become problematic for yourself and/or others. It can impact on how amicable a separation is or on the children involved. Anger may spill out into contact arrangements or co-parenting plans or any legal processes going on.

Anger can also exist outside of the grief process (we'll talk about anger as a standalone emotion in Chapter 2).

Bargaining

Bargaining in the context of the loss of a relationship/family/ perceived future, can look like this: hoping, wondering, persuading, begging, negotiating then bargaining. You might bargain with your ex-partner, with your faith and through prayer, or with yourself. This process happens as part of trying to find ways for this not to be the way this ends. You might suggest relationship counselling, you may offer to change or try to get your ex-partner to change, you might try to convince your ex-partner or yourself that things can be different. You might get caught up in the "what ifs" or "if onlys", ruminating over what could have been if only you had made different choices, different decisions, and so on.

> *When my ex left, I kept hoping that he would change his mind. I wanted things to go back to "normal", as I was so scared of this huge lifestyle change; so I told him I would change, and suggested counselling.* **Amy**

Depression

Depression can be heavy and overwhelming when the reality of the situation begins to set in and you realize the effect the relationship breakdown is going to have or is having on your life. It can include a whole range of emotions, including sadness, anxiety, fear, loneliness, guilt, numbness, emptiness and hopelessness. Depression can bring with it exhaustion, fatigue, inability to sleep, inability to get up, difficulty functioning, loss of appetite, rejection or avoidance of social activities or hobbies. It can make you think many negative thoughts about being alone, about the future, about your ability to cope, about how you see yourself. For more about depression, see Chapter 6;

for more about anxiety, see Chapter 5; for more about guilt, see Chapter 4.

Acceptance

Acceptance is the part of the process where you begin to come through the more difficult and intense emotions, and begin to reach a place of understanding and acknowledging the situation, and are thus able to begin to move forward with life in a meaningful way. This doesn't mean you won't continue to experience many of the emotions around grief, but they may be less intense, or you may have found ways to manage these once they show up. Acceptance means that you can begin to look forward and – gently and slowly – realize that you will be okay.

> It took a long time for me to accept the loss of the relationship, and even when I thought I was okay about it, something would happen and I'd suddenly be mourning the relationship again. It wasn't until I started doing more things for myself, like going to the gym, that I felt I was going to be okay. **Amy**

"GROWING AROUND GRIEF"

Alongside the stages of grief model there are other ways of understanding grief and loss that might make sense for you. Dr Lois Tonkin (a grief counsellor) has described a model of "Growing Around Grief". The idea of this model is that we learn to grow around our grief, so that over time, while the grief may always be present, we grow and grow around it, as we grow in ourselves and our new life, until we are much bigger than our grief, which can at first feel as big as us, if not bigger.

FOUR TASKS

A third way of capturing grief is through understanding the tasks of grief as described by psychologist Dr William Worden. These explain how we go through four tasks in our grief, (again, as with the stages of grief these can happen in any order, at any pace, and back and forward as needed). These tasks include:

- To accept the reality of the loss
- To experience and work through the pain and difficult emotions triggered by the loss
- To adjust to the new life
- To place the loss into the past, and to find a way forward investing in a new reality/life

Grief can ebb and flow over time, and for some, with time, it may pass completely; for others, it becomes something they learn to acknowledge and live with in a manageable way. There is no right or wrong way to experience grief, and everyone will experience it in their own way and in their own time, depending on the experience of the loss and what it meant for that individual.

WHAT MIGHT YOU BE GRIEVING?

Grief and loss as you come into single motherhood might involve any of the following losses (and sometimes more than one of these at once). Loss can be so individual, however, that you may experience other losses not mentioned here, or you may find some of these losses haven't affected you very much.

LOSS OF THE RELATIONSHIP

- Loss when a partner passes away
- Loss when a relationship ends while you are pregnant
- Loss when a relationship ends once the children are born
- Loss when a relationship ends due to infidelity
- Loss at the ending of a marriage/civil partnership/engagement/long-term relationship
- Loss of meaning and identifying as a couple

LOSS OF A TWO-ADULT HOUSEHOLD/ "TRADITIONAL FAMILY"

- Loss of a "typical family" set-up, identifying as a "traditional" family and becoming a single-parent family
- Loss of daily support – practically and/or emotionally
- Loss of companionship – someone to talk to/text/call daily
- Loss of daily contact/childcare with the children
- Loss of approval from friends or family (if they disapprove of you being a single parent or the way you came to be a single parent)

PRACTICAL LOSSES

- Loss of support in sharing daily tasks and responsibilities
- Loss of childcare support that comes from having the other parent in the household
- Loss of independent activity (for example, no longer able to take part in hobbies, as you no longer have the childcare)
- Loss of financial security
- Loss of the home you had or were planning to get

LOSSES OF THE FUTURE YOU HAD PLANNED

- Loss of not having more children

- Loss of the family future you had imagined, while also possibly seeing the future you had imagined play out with your ex-partner and their new partner/children

LOSS OF SOCIAL OPPORTUNITIES
- Loss of family holidays
- Loss of family Christmases/birthdays
- Loss of the social life as a family or couple

LOSSES RELATED TO OR THROUGH THE CHILDREN
- Grieving or supporting your child/children with loss of their parent from the household/becoming single-parent households
- Grieving or supporting your child/children with loss of traditional "family life"
- Getting used to your child spending time with your ex-partner and a new partner without you and, possibly, with their child/children

All of these are completely valid reasons to be grieving right now. You've been through a lot, and it's only natural to mourn what you thought would be. So be really, really kind to yourself, as you are likely to be grieving several losses at once, and that is tough.

GRIEF CAN AFFECT ANYONE

It's important to know that even if you might not be grieving all these losses, or even the big ones particularly, you might still experience grief and loss. And you can still experience grief and loss even if you are *not* mourning the loss of the relationship itself; for example, if you were the person to have left, or you agreed that the relationship ending was the right thing. You might still experience other losses though. You are human, and therefore may experience any of these elements of grief and loss, no matter the circumstances of the separation.

STORIES OF GRIEF AND LOSS IN SOLO MOTHERHOOD

Different experiences along this journey will impact on the nature of your grief and loss. We have described some of these below, with some amazing single parents sharing their stories. We will not have covered every experience, but hopefully we are able to give you some understanding to help you make sense of your own experience and to help you know you are not alone.

PREGNANT AND ALONE

While solo parenting is tough at the best of times, becoming a single mother before your child has even been born is a whole other ball game. You have to navigate all of those feelings of being a single parent while growing that baby on your own. You've got the solo hospital appointments, the uncomfortable nights in bed without anyone supporting you, and you don't get to enjoy any of the fun parts of being in a couple and having a baby – like choosing names together and getting excited about planning the nursery or buying cuddly toys or the pram together. Even if you are blessed with a great support system, you are this baby's main carer. To be faced with doing this alone can be incredibly scary and lonely. As such, you may begin grieving before your baby is born, and you may also experience grieving as you figure out the single motherhood journey once your baby arrives. And if your pregnancy was not planned, and so took your life on a very different route to what was expected, you're bound to grieve for the life you thought you would have.

Arabella, a single mum from York, thought she never wanted children; however, at 18 years old, and three months after she broke up with her ex, she found out she was pregnant.

"When I found out I was pregnant, I was in shock. I didn't think I could become a mum. I had my whole life ahead of me, and becoming a single mum when I wasn't even ready to become a mum was not in my plans."

After such a shock, Arabella deferred university and so had to cope with grieving the student life she had planned while replacing it with a very different lifestyle.

"What I struggled the most with was watching all my friends going to university and going on nights out while I was at home with a crying baby or dealing with a nappy explosion."

BREAKDOWN FROM INFIDELITY

An abrupt ending to a relationship is a real grief inducer, especially when infidelity is involved. It can be tough to process losing the person you loved and maybe thought you would be with forever while also coming to terms with the shock of betrayal and becoming a single parent. It's easy to get caught up in wondering why this happened. You might even have to experience seeing your ex with their new partner as you try to figure out your new path; or you may have to figure out your boundaries if your unfaithful partner tries to convince you not to leave. You will also still have to do normal day-to-day things while carrying around that heavy feeling of heartbreak, grief and loss.

Ellie became a single mum after her husband cheated on her, and she has only recently started to understand the breakdown of her relationship.

"I spent a long time thinking that he left me for the person he cheated on me with because I had become 'too much of a mum' and that I had lost my 'old self'; so I've spent a lot of time working on myself through therapy, and I now understand that his actions were not my fault."

Bella became a single mum when her husband walked out one day after 20 years of marriage.

"My husband was my best friend; we were together since we were teenagers and had two children together. One day he walked out, saying he didn't love me anymore. I found out from others that he had left me for someone else. I had no clue; I thought we were so strong. I was shocked, broken, scared. I worried when I went out that people were talking about me. I struggled to eat, I lost loads of weight, I lost so much confidence. Life changed overnight. I had to keep strong for the children, but daily activities were a struggle and sometimes I broke down. I was so worried for the children, who were devastated that their dad wasn't there and also upset at seeing me so sad. I was overwhelmed – it felt the way you feel when someone has died. I grieved having a husband, a partner, a friend, and having another parent and the children having their dad. It was so, so hard."

Emilia became a single mum in her 30s when her husband had an affair.

"We'd been together since we were young. Some aspects weren't perfect, but I certainly wouldn't have been the one to rock the boat. When the tsunami hit our marriage, I remember being in a bewildered state *for about six months. I just couldn't quite comprehend it had happened. It did feel like our marriage had died. It was a real loss. I was utterly heartbroken for me and my children."*

MISSING COMPANIONSHIP

After a relationship breaks down and you become a single mum, you may find yourself struggling with the loss of companionship – that constant person in your life who you can text, phone, expect to be there every day. When you are in a relationship, you have the implicit understanding that the other person is going to be there for you. If you have a problem, a bad day, an eventful day, the children do something challenging or funny, and all the other possible daily events in between, when you are in a relationship you have another person to share that with. When you become a single parent, suddenly that person isn't there anymore. And, however great your family and friends support system might be, they can't be there 24/7. And so this brings a loss, and a loneliness, which you have to process, grieve and adjust to.

*For **Katie**, becoming a single parent in her 40s with three children to look after was really tough. After being married for 25 years, the loss of the companionship was really hard.*

"When I separated I had a great support network of family and friends. I was actually quite confident I was going to be okay, however upset I was feeling. But the reality was so much harder than I imagined. I would have a tough day with work and the kids, and I would come home and there would just be no one to tell. I would be alone in the evenings after doing bedtime and there would be no one to chat with, have a glass of wine with, cuddle, or just watch TV with. I hadn't realized how much I had taken for

granted having that someone to talk to, and how much I needed that. Some days, after the break-up, I wouldn't speak to another adult! Not because I didn't want to or I didn't have friends and family, because I did – amazing ones who would always say to me to reach out. But the reality is they weren't there when I walked in from work, or had just finished bedtime. And I couldn't keep reaching out every time I experienced this feeling, which, to be honest was every day, all the time. And the loneliness of knowing that this was the reality of my life now, that I was alone now, in a way I hadn't been for 25 years, was really hard; I had to grieve the loss of that companionship. It is still hard now, but it is getting easier."

Filling the Companionship Gap

Try all or any of the following:

1. Acknowledge the reality of your new situation openly and honestly. Without a partner there is a gap in companionship that cannot be completely filled by friends and family. It's tough. It's real. And you don't have to gaslight yourself (or let others do this) by trying to convince yourself this isn't hard, or that there isn't something missing or that you would like.

2. Draw your Friendship Tree (inspired by Suzy Reading, author, coach and psychologist). Get a piece of paper and sketch out a tree shape. On the branches of the trees write the names of all the friends or family in your life – both close friendships and distant ones. Keep this drawing somewhere safe, and when you feel like you need to chat with someone or reach

out for company, get it out and remind yourself of the different people you could say hi to at this time. Don't be afraid to reach out and chat to people.

3. Plan ahead. Find new ways to occupy your time; anticipate the lonely times and come up with ideas and plans for long evenings or weekends when you miss company. This might involve seeing friends or family, doing DIY or completing a hobby, task, activity, new learning, exercise and much more.

4. Find other voices. Try listening to podcasts, audio books or radio shows that you might love. Listening to people chat away, especially if you listen regularly, forms a type of companionship that can fill quiet moments. Of course, this is only a one-way form of company, but it can bring humour, chat and entertainment into difficult times.

5. Consider ways to form new friendships, and of course when you are ready, new relationships. There are apps, social groups and new activities to try that would encourage this. There are so many social media accounts dedicated to supporting mums, and various Facebook groups you can join to meet other mums. There are also apps for single parents, such as Frolo, which is an app for single parents to meet other single parents in their area. In fact, this is how Amy met her now best friend; she moved to her village, befriended her on the app and they set up a playdate for their kids. The Bumble app also has an option to join just for friendships.

LOSS OF PRACTICAL HELP

When you realize there is no one to share the practical load with anymore, day to day, it can be overwhelming. There are no more "discussions" about who takes out the bins, no shared burden of housework, bedtimes or reading to the children. On *your* watch, it's your job; you can't hand it over because you're too tired or need to make a phone call or want to go for a run. If you don't do the task, it doesn't get done. And that's exhausting and frustrating, overwhelming and upsetting. More so if it's things you never did before – whether that is paperwork, finance management or DIY. Suddenly having to be responsible for doing all these things can be a constant reminder of what has gone and what is lost.

Jemma, a single mum of two in her late 30s described how she had to deal with the electricity going out in her new house a few months after she moved in.

"I sat and cried on the floor as I realized I didn't know how to deal with the problem on my own (I did work it out, but at the time this was my reaction). I felt silly asking someone and not knowing properly how to deal with the fuses or figure out the problem as I'd never had to do this before, because my ex had always sorted this. I also found bedtime every night exhausting, I was so tired I just wanted to cry at this point and was often snappy with the kids and then would feel terribly guilty. And then I'd come downstairs and have to empty the bins and hang up the washing and tidy the house and get the school clothes ready and feed the pets and hoover ... I'd get to bed exhausted, would barely sleep and then would get woken by the kids super early and start all over again."

GOODBYE FREEDOM

Becoming a single parent when your children are young can make the simplest of activities a struggle to achieve; whether it's a sporting activity, seeing friends, being able to pop to the shops or have some alone time outside of the house. Unless you have family or friends close by that are willing to help out with childcare, it's tough to find the opportunity to do things for yourself or to keep up old routines, hobbies and activities. If you're the primary caregiver of your child, you may get one night off a week or a fortnight (but sometimes not even that!), and with that added pressure of being the main one your child can go to, it's bound to take its toll.

> *When my relationship broke down, I really struggled with the loss of freedom. I get two weekends off a month, which is fine. What I miss terribly though is the evening yoga class on Mondays and being able to pop to the shop on my own – I'm absolutely screwed when I realize I've forgotten to buy milk for the morning, and my child is asleep.* **Amy**

Cleo was the one who left her ex-husband, and because she was the one to leave, she struggles to ask for help.

"I've always done something sporty and was heavily involved in Roller Derby, but all that had to come to a stop when we broke up. I've got no family close by, and I have never felt like I can ask my ex to have our daughter so I can do something for myself."

How to Help

It is really important to explore ways to find practical help and support that might be beyond the arrangements (formal and informal) that you may have made with your ex-partner.

It is important to recognize that you deserve time out from childcare responsibilities to do things that you know help you feel good and benefit your mental health, such as going to an exercise class, music class, art class, counselling session, or to an activity or task that had always been part of your life before the separation.

There will be tasks that you may have completed alone previously that you would still benefit from having time to do alone now. For example, some practical things will be far easier to do alone (for example, going to the doctor's, doing the "big shop", going to the tip, etc).

It is also really important to consider that, as you are now doing so much more as a solo parent, it is okay to ask others for help in ways you might not have done before. For example, help with school pick-ups, taking to after-school activities, help with evening care, DIY tasks, or anything else that you might not have needed help with before. Keep in mind that your capacity for these tasks may have changed post separation. You were not holding so much of the overall load before and so the situation is now different, and you deserve to have support.

Consider who you can ask for help and support. Remember that trying to do this all by yourself, or missing out on things, will inevitably negatively impact on your mental health and lead to resentment and frustration with your ex-partner or others who seem to have a much freer life. It will end up impacting negatively on yourself and your children if you become worn down. So, how can you get more help?

- Ask friends or family
- Consider childcare or wrap-around school care
- Consider being open and honest (amicably) with your ex-partner about what they need to do as a co-parent to continue to support you and your children
- Arrange mutual favours with friends

- Consider amending your and your children's activities, acknowledging you may not be able to do everything but prioritizing what is important for each of you

NO, THAT'S TOO MUCH FREEDOM!

Then there's the other end of the scale – you might not be the primary caregiver, or you might be sharing the children 50/50, and suddenly you have all of this free time. Going from spending every day with your children to only half that time or less can be devastating. Or even if you just have a free day, evening or weekend, that can suddenly be a huge shift.

> For **Katie** when she first had to have a day "off" from the children at the weekends, she really struggled.
> "Even though as a busy mum I'd often wish for time to myself, when I had to begin having days to myself while the kids were at their dad's I found it so difficult. There was something that really upset me, knowing that I only had this free time because my relationship (and family) had broken down. I struggled to enjoy the time. It was also hard because at weekends all my friends were with their families and I didn't feel I could intrude on anyone. So I had all this time but no idea how to spend it or enjoy it."

How to Help

You may have to find creative ways to cope with the new freedom and time that you find yourself with, while your children spend time with their other parent. Some of these ideas may help:

- Take your time. You will need time to adjust to having time to yourself, especially when you know the only reason you have this time is because of the relationship ending. Be gentle on yourself when you find this hard at first – it won't always be this way.

- Acknowledge the situation. Acknowledge all the thoughts and feelings this time alone brings. Acknowledge how it feels and name the emotion. Acknowledge why it bothers you – what feels difficult about this time. And remind yourself this will get easier with time.

- Plan ahead for how you can use this time. Make it meaningful, purposeful, aim to achieve something. Do something you enjoy. Do something you cannot do with your children present. Do something silly, adventurous, soothing, indulgent. Try something new. This is your time, and you can do what you want with it. Of course, this can be difficult to even think about or read about, and just doing so can trigger grief, guilt, anxiety, and every emotion in between. Be gentle with yourself. This can be tough.

- Don't feel like you have to persuade yourself (or let others persuade you) about how lucky you are to have this time. Of course, on the one hand the principle is true – for some people, having time to themselves is a rarity and luxury. But it doesn't mean you have to feel "lucky" just yet. It's okay that it doesn't feel good at first. Just take it one step at a time. And, in time, you might start to look forward to this freedom, to enjoy it, to value it, to be excited by it. And that is okay too. You can be an incredible mum and have all these feelings and more.

WHEN YOU'D HAVE LOVED MORE CHILDREN

Missing out on having more children is also a huge factor to get your head around, and not a simple thing to deal with. Amy always thought she would have more than one child, but the idea of getting into another relationship and potentially being left as a single mum with two children terrifies her! Another single mum, Sam, has similar feelings: "I wanted a sibling for my daughter and to be a mother again so badly, but I don't think I want this from my new life. It's a confusing thing to both want and not want something at the same time."

This is a theme that is common between single parents with just one child. Especially when you can see families with a child the same age start having second babies and growing their family. It can make you feel left out and like you're leaving too large a gap between your child and any potential future children. It can also be difficult if you have more than one child, but perhaps always hoped for a bigger family, or had been planning to try for a girl if you have two boys or vice versa, and so on. You may feel it is harder to achieve that dream now, or that you just don't want to achieve it with someone new. It can also be really hard if you feel like you should be giving your child a sibling – your child might even be asking for a brother or sister, making you feel terrible that you can't provide this right now. Whatever your experience, it can feel like a huge loss.

I have always loved the idea of having two children, but it just wouldn't work for me financially, emotionally or physically (there is not enough room in this house for any more humans!). My son wouldn't stop badgering me about wanting a little brother, and although I think he would be the best big brother there is, he needed to understand that it's not something that's on the cards for the moment. So, we settled for a bunny rabbit instead. Best compromise ever! **Amy**

MISSING THE FAMILY EXPERIENCE

It can also be really tough to have to give up the idea of giving your child the "typical family". Becoming a single mother means having to adjust both yourself and your child to a solo-parent household. Knowing that you cannot at this time offer your child a family set-up with two loving parents at home can be heartbreaking.

> My son's dad's new partner has her own children, and whenever he stays at their house, he spends a lot of time with two other children as well as his dad and a motherly figure. It's been pretty tough seeing them spending time all together as a family, and although I'm happy that he has a great relationship with them, I still grieve the fact I can't give him that same set-up at home. And I know I'm not the only one that feels like this. **Amy**

Ellie struggles with herself potentially running out of time to have more children, whereas her ex-husband is already in a new relationship.

"It hurts when I think that her dad could go on to have more children and give her that family experience. Also, that she might prefer to spend her time with her 'dad family' rather than just being with her mum with no children to play with."

PICTURE-PERFECT PARENTING

All of a sudden, you are a single parent and there are families, couples, happy parents and children everywhere. It can be heartbreaking to see two-parent households doing things together. Whether it's at the supermarket, the park, on Facebook, you suddenly seem to be bombarded with images of the family and the relationship you are missing. Amy felt this most in the early days of her break-up, as it was just before Christmas and the whole of social media was filled with happy family photos!

Jemma talked about her experiences:

"After we separated it felt like all I could see were couples, families all together. Anytime I received an invite that was open to couples or families it would make my heart sink. Happy family photos on social media were always painful! Some days it would be like the grief hitting me all over again. It would feel like being punched in the stomach at times, or I'd feel it in my chest and I'd cry in the car park or on my walk home."

Even once you have mourned your relationship, you may still grieve being able to do family days out with another adult, family holidays and celebrating birthdays and Christmases together. When Amy and her ex first broke up and her ex started seeing someone else, she felt completely broken when her son went on a day trip to the beach with them all. For Amy, it felt like she was being left out of her own family. However, it helped when she reminded herself you might fantasize about doing all these family things, when in reality they may not be that great – there might be bickering or trauma over lost toys or someone gets ill. And if the relationship is not working, then these family days may not be full of fun, laughter and happy memories.

MONEY WORRIES

Let's talk about money ... or the lack thereof! We all know the age-old saying of money doesn't buy us happiness, which we agree with – to some extent. However, whoever said that doesn't understand the sadness and fear that comes with not being able to afford your gas bill, relying on your ex-partner's child maintenance payment to come through so you can buy bread, or living pay check to pay check hoping that you'll make it to next month without maxing out your overdraft or credit card. Even on a good salary, in today's expensive world, going from a two-salary household to a one-salary household (even with child maintenance) can be really hard.

Grieving the loss of your family and then the loss of your financial security on top of this can be really tough and scary. Trying to cope with everything *and* juggle finances or negotiate financial settlements can often trigger anger and resentment too. You might be afraid your settlement won't be enough, feel hopeless about how on earth you will manage, or angry and resentful that your ex may not be carrying the same burdens. Anger around these issues can also come from ex-partners being resentful of having to pay maintenance or other cost-related issues. Frankly, this is a hotbed of conflict waiting to happen.

> **Amanda** *took her three teenage children and left her relationship of 25 years to move into a rented property nearby. While she is so much happier now, she is struggling to cope with the financial problems that have occurred.*
>
> *"I grieve for the financial security that my old life had compared to how tight things are now on my own. We owned the house we were living in, so we didn't have too many financial worries as a couple. Moving out as a self-employed single mum with three kids completely flipped my life upside down."*

Amanda raises an additional pressure here – being self-employed and becoming a single parent has an extra level of stress as you are responsible for your earnings: if you don't work, you don't get paid. So whereas you might have been able to take time off easily for school sports days or when the children were sick, it suddenly becomes much harder when money becomes tighter. A lack of financial security can also make you feel guilty for not being able to afford expensive gifts and holidays for your child – not necessarily because you wish you could spoil them, but there is an emotional drain that comes with not being able to afford to provide our children with something they would love.

Finding practical financial support will be really important, and is something you may have to figure out in the midst of your grief. Seek professional advice and support for this, as dividing up money and assets can be tricky, as can figuring out how you will survive financially on one salary and what you are entitled to.

For readers in the UK, the following may be helpful:

- The charity Gingerbread (www.gingerbread.org.uk) can help you find grants and other financial support.
- The government-run website MoneyHelper (www. moneyhelper.org.uk, formerly the Money Advice Service) simply explains Universal Credit and what you could be entitled to.
- Child Maintenance – the government website (www.gov. uk/calculate-child-maintenance) has a simple calculator for checking how much maintenance you should receive from your ex-partner. You are entitled to this maintenance, so it is important that you seek legal support if disputes arise regarding your ex's financial contributions.

For readers in the US, the following may be helpful:

- Single Mother Guide (www.singlemotherguide.com) can help you work out what financial assistance you might be entitled to.
- Single Mothers Grants (www.singlemothersgrants.org) features a directory of grants for single mothers.

Katie explained that she and her ex-partner sought advice together from a mediator who helped advise *on the process of separating and dividing up money and assets.*

"It was an awful process, and I remember crying most of the way through each meeting, as every conversation triggered my grief and loss, and I was immensely sad. This is when I found out we were getting divorced straight away. But, however distressing it was, we were both clear we wanted to sort out the finances fairly and without conflict, and the mediator helped give us answers we just didn't have and helped us through this fairly and relatively quickly. We also used the child maintenance website to calculate the child maintenance, which was really helpful."

FINDING WAYS TO MANAGE AND COPE WITH GRIEF

So now that we understand a bit more about grief and loss and the ways these show up in solo motherhood, what can we do when we feel this way? In this last part of the chapter, we've shared some ideas that can be helpful when grief and loss is in your life. There is also an exercise at the end of this chapter to help you make sense of your own experiences of grief and loss, and what you can do to help.

There is no set way to cope with grief. To a certain extent, it is important to know that the grief process is a natural process; there is nothing wrong with you for grieving. There is no set time limit on grieving. Grief will inevitably move and change as time progresses. If we allow ourselves to feel it and process it, we can allow it to flow through us, and eventually it will lessen or move on. However, there are some things we can do to help ourselves along the way, to ease the pain a little and help things move toward a brighter future.

ALLOW YOURSELF TIME

There is no set timeline on grief. There is no set pattern or way that it will show up, or then fade from your life. Your path is unique – it will not be the same as that of your friends, your parents, or your ex-partner. Your grief process will be what it will be. Give yourself time to grieve, and give yourself time to come *through* your grief. However, watch out for grief becoming *stuck*: if you start to find it becomes difficult to function, your relationships begin to suffer, and you feel stuck in the grief you are feeling. It can be worth taking extra steps to seek support to help work through your grief, (see "Make Space to Talk" page 30).

MAKE SPACE FOR GRIEF

This is a difficult idea, as you may want to push away your grief (and all its associated emotions), but finding a way to make space for our grief – to breathe into our grief, to turn toward it rather than resisting it, fighting it or pushing it away – is a powerful way of helping grief move through and, over time, subside. This concept comes from Acceptance and Commitment Therapy, or ACT.

Turn Toward Your Grief

1. Take a moment when you notice feelings of grief rising up.
2. Take a slow, deep breath and name the emotion(s) you are feeling and where you feel this in your body.
3. Take another slow, deep breath, and imagine breathing into the feeling/physical sensation; as you breathe, imagine you are making space around the feeling.

4. Acknowledge that this is grief showing up right now – it is painful and upsetting and, while you wish you didn't have to feel it, it is here and you can manage it.

5. Take the next small step. Focus on whatever you need to, despite the grief being here. Take a moment to cry, pause, text a friend, go for a walk, blast some music, have a cuddle with your child, write down how you are feeling, finish your chores, or whatever is the best next step you can take right now.

6. If these feelings are intense and overwhelming, you can use a technique called "dropping anchor", which aims to help you stay grounded and anchored in the midst of an emotional storm. You can find audio clips by Dr Russ Harris for this technique at www. actmindfully.com.au/free-stuff/free-audio/.

MAKE SPACE TO TALK

Talking about your grief and loss is really important. You do not have to keep this bottled up. No matter the circumstances of the end of your relationship and how you became a single mother, it is okay to talk. To begin with you can choose to talk to friends or family members. These are a wonderful source of support. However, it is important to be mindful that friends or family cannot take responsibility for containing our grief completely; they can become overwhelmed if we share every moment of our grief. So, if you feel like you need more support than perhaps one friend or family member can carry by themselves, then it may help to consider other avenues of talking support, such as:

- Talk to lots of different friends and family members over time
- Contact a helpline or text line (for example, Relate in the UK offer a variety of text and chat options or Shout is a text support crisis line)
- Speak to a relationship counsellor or seek therapy support from a counselling or clinical psychologist or other professional specifically trained in grief and/or family/relationship difficulties

Jemma says:

"It helped me in my grief to see a therapist. I kept getting overwhelmed and crying. I didn't want to keep turning to my friends. I went to see a relationship counsellor early on and just talked and cried and shared what was happening. A bit later in the process I went back again and talked to a counselling psychologist. There was lots of crying again, but it felt so good to talk to someone separate from my friends and family. Also I got some really helpful advice about reconnecting with friends, and some reassurance that it was okay to feel what I was feeling."

WRITE THINGS DOWN

It can help to write down or journal how you feel. This can help you let out your thoughts and feelings, and can help you make sense of everything going on in your mind. This can also help you see how things change over time. *The Joy of Writing Things Down* by Megan C Hayes is a wonderful book that explains all the different ways we can use writing or journaling to help with how we feel in a range of situations.

PRACTISE KIND SELF-TALK

Over time as you process your grief, you may wish to find some resilient, calming, soothing self-talk that you can use when things get hard. For example, you could say to yourself things like: "This is hard, but with time this will get easier." "It is going to be better in the long run to not be in an unhappy relationship." "The children/my child will adapt and cope with support." "It's okay to find this difficult; it's okay to grieve." "One day I can explore having a relationship again, and it's okay to not want this now."

TAKE CARE OF YOURSELF

Taking care of yourself is so, so, *so* important. We can't stress this enough. This can be self-care through looking after yourself practically; taking care in getting washed, dressed, brushing your hair, wearing your favourite clothes; taking care to eat and drink well, to get some sleep, or take exercise; taking care to see friends, do hobbies and more.

Care can also be talking kindly to yourself and practising self-compassion. We will talk about all these ideas more in the following chapters. You deserve to take care of yourself, so repeat this to yourself, please: "I deserve care."

ADDICTIVE SUBSTANCES

Please take care that, during this grieving time, you do not rely too heavily on comfort eating, alcohol or drugs to cope with or numb your grief and loss. For some this may be really tempting if this is your go-to way to cope with difficult emotions. But this will only make the process more difficult. So, where possible, try to keep addictive substances within moderate/minimal use. If you are struggling with this, please do seek therapy help and support.

STAY ACTIVE

No matter how heavy the grief gets, try to keep moving. Try to get outside, into your garden or local park, or even just step outside of your home. Go for a walk, take up some exercise or sport. Getting some fresh air and moving more can, either in combination or individually, positively impact mood and wellbeing; so give yourself the best chance to feel okay by including these in your day. For single-mum Bella, *"running was my saviour, it kept me sane"*.

REFOCUS

When we acknowledge and make space for our grief, we can then also begin to allow ourselves to gently refocus on the here and now – on what we still have and what we can still do. We can draw our focus to what is the next thing we can do – the next meaningful step that will help us continue to live our life according to the person we are and want to be. We can focus on what may make us feel good, what may help lift us up, energize us, soothe us. We can focus on activities or hobbies, or being around people that can help. In time, we can take part in gratitude practices to draw our attention to what we can still be grateful for; this may be hard at times, but not impossible.

CARRYING ON

In 2020 the broadway actor Nick Cordero sadly passed away due to Covid in America. His wife and widow, Amanda Kloots, was left alone as a single mother to their young son. One of the tasks Amanda set herself shortly after Nick's death was to take up a brand-new hobby. She chose tennis, and began to find joy through learning this new skill every week. In her book *Live Your Life*, Amanda talks candidly about how her grief was still present, yet she was able to focus on this activity alongside her grief. For anyone trying to make sense of living through and surviving the death of a partner as a parent, this is a powerful book.

We hope this chapter has given you an insight into grief and loss and how you can get through this tough time. To help you reflect on your experiences, Dr Emma has put together an exercise for you to undertake to help you make sense of your experiences of grief and loss.

Reflections on Your Experience of Grief and Loss

1. Take a moment, grab a pen and piece of paper if you can, and reflect on (and write down) the losses you have experienced through your journey to solo motherhood.
2. What have you felt as you experienced or still experience these losses? Name all the emotions. This could include: anxiety, sadness, fear, guilt, shame, anger, rage or frustration.
3. What triggers your feelings of grief and loss (this could be people, events, sounds, places, etc.)?
4. How have your experiences of grief and loss changed since your separation first began?

5. What have you found has helped you when you have experienced this grief and loss? What has been unhelpful?

6. What ideas have you found in this chapter that can help you?

2

RAGE, ANGER AND FRUSTRATION

So, your world has done a full 180 – and you are MAD. Incredible Hulk MAD. Whether it was a messy break-up, there was infidelity, or you're simply fuming because your ex took the coffee machine (yes, Amy's ex had the audacity to do that), you may be feeling all kinds of anger and rage.

WHAT DO WE MEAN BY ANGER AND RAGE?

Anger is a normal, healthy human emotion. We will all feel degrees of anger at times in our life. Anger can be directed at ourselves, at others or at the situation in general. And sometimes it is misdirected; for example, it is directed at others when really it is the situation we are mad at, or it can be directed at others when really we are angry with ourselves.

Anger has different levels of intensity: annoyed, frustrated, irritated, angry, furious, raging, wrathful.

Anger can be triggered by themes of injustice and unfairness; by feeling violated, threatened, out of control, vulnerable, shamed, humiliated, not good enough, insignificant or uncared for. Tiredness, stress, worry and burnout can also trigger anger.

Anger is often present on the surface and can mask many emotions that may be present below the surface. Anger may be present when really, deep down, we feel pain, sadness, hurt, betrayal, grief, fear, shame or devastation. Imagine an iceberg: the tip of the iceberg (above the water) is the anger and rage, but the much larger part of the iceberg below the surface is filled with a whole range of other emotions.

Anger activates the fight or flight system in your body causing a spike in adrenalin, which prepares your body for "fight" and makes us feel strong (the "Hulk" phenomenon). Psychologically, we can understand anger in terms of: how it makes us feel (the emotion), how it makes us feel physically (bodily symptoms), how it makes us think (thoughts, memories) and how it makes us act (behaviours, how we communicate).

WHAT TRIGGERS OUR ANGER?

When we experience anger after a relationship breakdown and at the beginning of the journey into solo motherhood, the anger can be primal, intense, overwhelming. You are trying to make sense of a whole range of emotions and through that process it can be easy to become tipped over into anger and rage. Often these anger and rage emotions can feel "safer" to become lost in, rather than having to really feel and experience all the other painful emotions under the surface.

The anger and rage can be triggered in several ways.

Anger may spark once you realize that the relationship is, indeed, over, and there is absolutely nothing you can do about it – especially if the relationship didn't end on your terms or you can't understand what led to it. Ultimately, this sense of powerlessness and lack of control can trigger anger (to read more about powerlessness and control see Chapter 7).

Anger may also be triggered when you face new circumstances because of the break-up (for example, not being invited to a social event that your ex-partner is attending) or when everyone else in your social group can easily go out for the evening as their partners can cover childcare, while you are realizing you cannot do that anymore. It may also be when your child asks for their other parent and not you.

You may feel anger when the burden of parenting responsibility falls too much on you.

The anger and rage may arise when you are trying to negotiate finances or separating out your belongings, or when you experience your ex-partner as being unhelpful or uncaring.

Whatever the reason, it is easy for anger and rage to simmer and boil over.

As time passes, the anger may begin to simmer down – it can still be there, but it may be more controlled, muted, less intense, less primal. However, as new situations arise in your solo-motherhood journey – new milestones or moments of change/adjustment – then it can be possible for anger and rage to be triggered freshly and intensely all over again.

Anger might be triggered again a few months into solo motherhood, or a few years. It might be triggered when your ex-partner finds a new partner, or gets engaged, marries or has a new baby. It may be when your children talk about all the great times they had on holiday with your ex-partner when you can't afford this for your children; or it may be when you are just exhausted with the constant childcare, responsibility and demands on you as a single mum.

COMMON TRIGGERS FOR ANGER AFTER A BREAK-UP AND IN SOLO PARENTING

- Disagreements about co-parenting
- Inequalities in childcare or financial responsibilities
- A sense of unfairness about an aspect of the situation
- Being taken for granted

- Feeling trapped in parenting duties and unable to do what you used to do
- When your ex moves on
- Being on the receiving end of controlling or aggressive/ threatening behaviour
- When you feel like other people (friends or family) forget/ don't understand how difficult solo parenting is
- When family events are planned socially, and you don't feel like a "family"
- When your co-parent does things that you don't agree with or feel are right, but which are out of your control

STORIES OF ANGER IN SOLO MOTHERHOOD

BEING ANGRY AT YOURSELF

You might be angry at yourself – feeling like you weren't good enough or you could have done something to keep your family together.

Perhaps you chose to end the relationship and you're angry that you couldn't make it work for your child's sake. But remember – while it's lovely for people to work things out and live as a two-adult household, if your heart wasn't in it, your heart wasn't in it. No amount of forcing yourself would have made things better, and if you decided to stay together for the sake of the children, you probably would have done more damage than good. You will have made the decision to leave based on myriad good reasons. Remember these when self-directed anger toward yourself comes calling.

Amanda stayed with her ex-husband for over 10 years longer than she would have liked for the children's sake. However, when discussing the situation with her she explained:

"Staying with him for the sake of the kids affected not only me but the kids. By the end of the relationship, they had even started asking why I hadn't left him yet."

BEING ANGRY AT YOUR EX

Even if it was an amicable break-up, chances are you will feel some level of anger toward your ex. More so if infidelity was involved, or you feel let down or betrayed. Thinking about them is probably stirring up some angry feelings right now.

It is natural to find someone to blame when you're hurt. And, while your anger is totally valid, it's likely that holding on to this anger is not helping you.

*When **Jemma** first separated from her ex-partner she was so angry all the time.*

"I could barely face looking at my ex, let alone talking to him. Handovers with the children were really hard; I hated being there with all this simmering anger. I was angry he left; angry the children were without their family; angry life seemed easy for him (I've no idea if it was or not); angry he didn't see the children much, even though I encouraged it; angry everything seemed my responsibility. I would struggle to reply to messages as the anger was so strong. Occasionally, I would snap and react angrily in person or on a message, but for the most part I tried to contain it. But it was there, simmering away, every day."

INFIDELITY

Being cheated on sucks. You put your faith and trust into another human being, and they go and shatter that. You're left wondering, why did they do it? How could they? What does the other person have that you don't? So many questions, which you're unlikely to get answers to.

*When **Ellie** found out her ex was moving in with the woman he cheated on her with she had the urge to phone her.*

"I felt a rush of anger and told her what a huge responsibility this was, and that she must ensure that her house was safe for my daughter to live in. I told her of the duty of care that she had, and reiterated that if she was going to be around my daughter as a step-mum figure then she would be a role model and she should not take that lightly! When I put the phone down, I felt like I could have had a heart attack! I was just in full-on protection mode!"

Perhaps it would be best if technology could take a hike when we're fuming! When Amy found out her son had met her ex's new girlfriend, she went ballistic. A flurry of grammatically incorrect ANGRY TEXTS WITH CAPITAL LETTERS ensued ... because that's the ideal way to release anger, right? Nope! Angry texts are best avoided – you can't unsend those bad boys!

CO-PARENTING RAGE

Some of you may have been dealing with rage-inducing co-parenting moments since the moment your child was born.

*When **Arabella** told her ex-boyfriend she was pregnant he promised he would be present and support her. What happened was very different.*

"Within an hour of my son being born, he left the hospital and I didn't see him for a year. I bumped into him on my first night out and he looked at me like he didn't even know me. My friend had to send me home because, I swear, I would have ended up in a police car if I had spoken to him!"

Arabella's situation is horrible. But even if your ex is "active" in your child's life, you may still have issues. Co-parenting is bloody hard.

Katie would often find herself getting frustrated with the smallest co-parenting interactions.

"I would find myself getting so angry when clothes were brought home unwashed, homework was forgotten, or I'd have to pack my children snacks for school as their dad wouldn't bother to buy any. It would drive me crazy. I began to learn that my anger showed up in any situation that made me want to scream 'It's not just my job!'"

Dealing with the disappointment of your child's other parent playing such a small role in their life is infuriating. You can see how amazing your child is and think they deserve so much better than what their other parent is giving them.

*What **Arabella** finds the hardest now is that her son's dad is constantly in and out of his life.*

"I've become used to his dad being flaky, but it never gets easier. It was his turn to go to football practice and he just didn't turn up to pick up our son. The football coach ended up driving him home to me. What makes me so mad is that he's letting his son down over and over again."

Unfortunately, some people are unreliable, there is nothing you can do to force them to support and care for your child like you wish they would. If you can't get through to them, it's their loss. While you probably want to shout at them or send them a flurry of angry messages, the best thing you can do is to step back, talk to someone else, lean on your friends for support, as it's unlikely you'll ever get through to them, especially when you are angry.

Your top priority is your child's best interests, so when these situations occur, instead of harnessing your energy into anger toward your ex, try to look at how, although they've been let down again, your child still has you. The fact you get so angry when your child is let down shows how strong a bond you have. Even though you may have a few explicit words you'd like to say to the other parent, It is best to take a breath, blow out the anger, and keep calm and collected. In the long run, this will be best for you and your child.

Seeing someone else letting your child down is such an angering thing. We care for and protect these babies, so when someone lets them down it brings out the protective mama bear in us; not to mention we're the ones who have to deal with the fallout from the child being let down.

Frankie's ex was due to collect her daughter from school but was running late and didn't let her know.

"I had to go and get her; she was the last kid left in the playground with a teaching assistant, and she cried and asked me why I wasn't there. She knew it was her weekend with him, but as I was the one that turned up she was really upset with me. If he had just told me he would be late I could have collected her on time."

ANGER AT SOCIAL LIFE CHANGES

It's hard to come to terms with how things change once you become a single parent. Mutual friends have to figure out how to be with you *and* with your ex, couples' activities become tricky now it's just you, family get-togethers with other families may change because you aren't a typical two-parent "family" anymore.

The anger and frustration at these changes in your life can be common, whether that anger is directed at yourself or at (not entirely rationally) the friends, couples or families that may change their behaviours (and invites) when you become a single mum.

For **Katie**, this was something she really struggled with.

"When I became a single parent, I didn't really anticipate friendship issues. As it was, it turned out there was plenty to trigger anger and frustration (and a lot of sadness underneath). I lost a good friend, who chose to stick with my ex-partner and not me because my ex was more 'fun' than I was after the separation (I was really struggling). I found that family and, of course, couples invites stopped, and while solo or 'mums with kids' invites did happen, the anger at feeling 'rejected' from these family invites because I was now a single parent was really upsetting."

ANGER BECAUSE YOU ARE JUST SO TIRED AND SOLO PARENTING IS HARD

Sometimes you find anger and irritation creeping in because you are just so bloody tired. You are exhausted. You've worked all day. You've parented. You've tidied the house. It gets to bedtime and no one will listen and go to bed. You lose your temper, shout, cry, snap. The children go to bed on a grumpy note. You go to bed feeling terrible. It's a rubbish end to a long, long day.

This scenario is really common. When you are tired, stressed, feeling all the pressures and burdens of single parenthood, it is fairly common to be snappy, irritable, impatient, intolerant of situations. And, let's face it, single motherhood is mostly full of moments of feeling really tired and having too much to do and not enough time to do it in.

Jemma noted:

"I'd often find myself snapping at the kids. They would shout mummy one too many times; they would expect to be waited on while they watched TV; they were used to not having to do many chores, and now as a single mum

I needed them to help a bit more, and would get so cross when they would leave their cup on the side, or their plate on the sofa, or leave their school shoes lying about. Trouble is, I was really inconsistent. Because I liked being that mum who looked after them and cared for them and let them relax, but then every now and then I would just snap and shout, and the poor things didn't know what was expected of them. But this was me and my anger, because I was so stressed and tired and worn out with too much to do."

UNDERSTAND YOUR ANGER AND RAGE

Understanding our anger can be the first step to helping ourselves manage it, soothe it or respond differently to it. First, we can understand what triggers our anger, and then we can understand the thoughts, feelings, physical symptoms and behaviours we experience once anger is triggered.

TRIGGERS
Triggers could be external – for example, events, behaviours, things other people say or do – or internal – for example, thoughts, images or memories about your situation, your relationship, being a single parent and so on. It is also useful to keep in mind that there are factors that might not be direct anger triggers, but that may make you more likely to be irritable or angry, such as having not slept, tiredness, being in physical pain, dealing with other emotions, having too much to do and so on.

THOUGHTS
Our thoughts play an important part in fuelling or maintaining our anger. When anger is triggered it is helpful to work out: What do you think about the situation you are in? What thoughts do you have about yourself, your ex-partner, others, your future,

your past, your current life in solo motherhood? What images or memories come into your mind?

Here are five crucial points about thoughts that we will return to in other chapters of this book:

1. The way we think about our situation influences how we feel and how we behave.
2. Thoughts are not facts. They are interpretations/ perspectives on a situation, influenced by our experiences, our mood, our past beliefs.
3. Our thinking is not always rational, reasonable, accurate, evidence-based or fair.
4. When we experience high emotion, our thinking can be biased, faulty, irrational, inaccurate.
5. When we believe our thoughts without question, and then base how we feel and behave on these thoughts, we can end up in tricky situations – and can often end up making situations worse for ourselves and others.

Common Thinking Biases in Anger

When we think about situations we are all prone to making "thinking errors" or having unhelpful biases in our thinking. If these biases in our thinking go unchecked, they can ramp up our anger and rage, so trying to be aware of the presence of these biases can be really important.

When we are angry we can do any of the following (these are some examples, and not an exhaustive list!):

- Think in *black and white* (ie, all good or all bad). These are often big, final, no room for negotiation, all or nothing statements, such as: "I will never forgive them".
- Make *assumptions* and *mind-read*. We assume we know what another person is thinking or why they did something; for example, "They (ex-partner) don't care

47

about me" or "People must think I'm useless because my marriage broke down".

- *Predict the future.* We think our future is set in stone; for example, "I'm never going to have a happy family again".
- Engage in *emotional reasoning.* We think that because we *feel* something it must be true; for example, "I *feel* like no one (my ex, my family, my friends) cares about me".
- *Overgeneralize.* We make blanket statements or transfer a conclusion from one situation to every situation; for example, "No one is never going to love me", "My ex-partner never helps with the children", "Being a single parent means I can never go out".

FEELINGS

When anger is triggered what emotions do you feel? How can you best describe the feeling, and not just the anger but the feelings underneath the anger?

PHYSICAL SYMPTOMS

When anger is triggered what physical symptoms do you notice in your body? Do you feel tension, headaches, tight chest, hot, sweaty, heart racing, etc? We know that when we feel angry and our body is in fight or flight mode, it activates a range of physical symptoms.

BEHAVIOURS

When anger is triggered how do you behave? What urges and impulses do you have? What do you want to say and do and what *do* you say and do?

Often, without support or strategies to manage our anger effectively, our behaviour when triggered by anger can be uncontrolled, impulsive, reactive or aggressive/passive aggressive. When we go into that fight or flight mode we are in a very primitive place where we may be prone to lashing out physically or verbally (fight mode), or doing something dramatic to take ourselves out of the situation or just withdrawing (flight mode). If we *react* (uncontrolled) to anger and behave impulsively, or if we learn to *respond* (controlled, calm, considered) to our anger then the behaviours we see may be very different.

React Aggressively

We can be aggressive in our words, our body language or our actions. This can include verbal aggression: shouting and/or screaming, making abusive, unpleasant, cruel comments); and physical aggression: hitting, punching, kicking people or damaging or destroying objects.

React Passive Aggressively

We can be passive aggressive when we communicate our anger in indirect ways – sulking, ignoring, "ghosting" (blocking/unfollowing someone on social media or text/phone), saying "I'm fine/It's fine" while clearly communicating it isn't through our tone, body language, and so on.

Respond Assertively

We can be assertive by expressing our anger clearly, calmly, rationally (more about this later in the chapter).

Take a moment to think about how you tend to communicate and express your anger – are you usually assertive, aggressive or passive aggressive?

Please know – it is not unusual to feel intense rage at times during the journey into single motherhood and, because of that, intense urges to physically hurt someone or something. It is not unheard of to instinctively want treasured possessions to be broken, clothes to be thrown onto the street, or to march around and bang on doors, and scream, shout and rage.

Of course, it's never advised to act on this rage, as it will only bring more challenges, conflict and complications, as well as remorse, shame and guilt when the rage begins to die away. If you feel this way, keep reading for healthy ways to release this rage without causing any actual harm.

REACTION VERSUS RESPONSE

Reacting in Anger	Responding Calmly When Angry
Verbal reaction:	*Verbal response:*
Shout	Count to ten (in your head)
Scream	Speak at a normal volume and in a normal tone of voice
Argue	
Accuse	Explain how you feel using "I", not "You" statements
Threaten	
Ignore conversation/refuse to talk	Explain if you need a break, are finding it hard to talk, or need time to take on board what they have said
	Ask the other person's opinion/perspective – listen
	Be open to finding a resolution
Physical reaction:	*Physical response:*
Throw things	Breathe deeply
Break things	Stay outwardly calm
Attack someone	Walk away for a break if you need to, ideally expressing this verbally before doing so, and always coming back to discuss once calmer
Non-verbal body language:	*Non-verbal body language:*
Clench fists	Positive eye contact
Tighten jaw	Arms down
Fold arms	Hands open
Stare or refuse to make eye contact	Sit down, if possible

See Your Anger

Think about a recent situation as a solo parent that triggered your anger, and write down your answers to the following questions.

1. What triggered your anger?
2. What were you thinking in that situation?
3. How did you feel in that situation? Try to think about the emotions on the surface (the angry ones) and the emotions underneath the surface.
4. What physical symptoms did you notice?
5. How did you behave in this situation? Were you aggressive, passive aggressive or assertive?

Katie went through an exercise for us and identified the following:

Trigger: "Despite being amicable and doing lots of things together socially since the separation, unexpectedly (for me) my ex-partner had a get-together with mutual friends of ours, including some of my best friends, with mums, dads, children, and didn't invite me."

Thoughts: "I had lots of thoughts, including about being excluded; that my ex didn't care about me, or didn't want me there; that my friends didn't care about me enough to not go without me, or to ask for me to be invited; that I didn't matter. I had thoughts about the future, about whether this was how it would be from now on, not being invited to things my friends were going to. I had memories about when we had all hung out together as families. I had lots of images in my head about what the social occasion was like without me."

SURVIVING SOLO MOTHERHOOD

Feelings: "I was angry. I was raging, actually. I was so, so furious. I was angry at my ex-partner and I was a bit angry at my friends. Underneath the anger, I was sad, hurt, disappointed; I felt let down, and a little bit betrayed. I felt hopeless about the future."

Physical symptoms: "I had a terrible headache, I felt like I had been crying for days, and I had a really tight feeling in my chest."

Behaviours: "I wasn't particularly proud of my behaviour at first. I went through being aggressive, then passive aggressive, then eventually (and only just) assertive. I shouted at my ex-partner. I then refused to speak to him. I withdrew from my friends. I withdrew from the world for a day and stayed home, cancelling social plans. After a few days of letting my anger die down (and spending time using exercises my therapist had given me to work through my anger and calm it down), I had a calmer conversation with my ex-partner and I reconnected with my friends. I adjusted my expectations for future social activities, and understood that this new stage would mean we would start doing more things separately."

SUPPORTING YOURSELF THROUGH ANGER AND RAGE

When you feel anger and rage, one thing you can do is look at how you can calm and soothe yourself and your anger before you decide how to respond. This will not prevent you from tackling the issues that have made you angry, but will give you the best chance of responding in a helpful and effective way.

IMMEDIATE CRISIS ANGER MANAGEMENT

If you are feeling angry and raging at a situation it could be tempting to express this straight away – to your ex-partner, your children, your friends or family, or colleagues. However, when you do this, there is a high chance you may express your anger in ways that may be intense, volatile, aggressive or passive aggressive, which increases the chance the person your anger is directed at will respond in kind and the situation may escalate. Or you may direct your anger at people immediately closest to you. Either way it can end up being destructive.

Emergency Strategies

Try these crisis strategies to help you contain your anger long enough for you to calm down and decide with a clearer head how you want to deal with the anger-inducing situation.

- It's an old adage, but count to ten! This helps to slow down your response, and creates a break between the situation and your response. Count to 50 if you need!
- Take a deep breath; then another if you need to (see page 126).
- Imagine a traffic light system: on red your anger is boiling, and you need to wait before you respond; on amber the anger is reducing in intensity and you can start thinking about how to respond; on green you can go and respond more calmly.
- Walk away, take some time out, go into another room, take yourself out of the situation. If you can, explain, "I need to take a minute, I can't talk right now", so that you give people the chance to give you space.
- Use a grounding/dropping anchor strategy (see page 31); push your feet into the floor, press your hands together, stand up straight, focus on anchoring yourself while you try any of the above strategies.

Anger-management Strategies

Once the crisis level of anger has subsided, try the following when you have some time to work on your anger and reflect.

1. Acknowledge and name how you are currently feeling about the situation. Are you angry, raging, furious? Or are you experiencing annoyance, irritation, frustration? Research shows that naming our emotion helps us to deal with it more effectively.
2. Once you have named the anger, see if you can delve deeper and notice what emotions are going on for you under the anger. Are you sad, hurt, disappointed, feeling betrayed, feeling scared and so on? If you struggle to do this at this stage, see if you can do this after step 4.
3. See if you can notice where in your body you are holding the anger, the tension, the rage. You might find it helpful to move around, stretch, walk, shake your body, shake out the tension. Sometimes it helps to clench and unclench the muscles (for example, in your hands, your shoulders, your jaw). This type of exercise is called progressive relaxation.
4. Take some deep breaths. There is so much power in calming deep breaths. We know that when we are angry our fight or flight system is activated. This is located in the part of our nervous system called the sympathetic nervous system. However, when we take slow, deep breaths we activate the other part of our nervous system called the parasympathetic nervous system; this is where our rest, relax, digest system is, where we can soothe ourselves and calm ourselves. When in fight or flight mode, we are agitated and tense; taking deep breaths is one way of calming down the physical response in the body. See the breathing exercise in Chapter 5 for further ideas.
5. Practise mindfulness to notice your thoughts (and other aspects of the anger process). There is a great YouTube

video by Happify that explains the use of mindfulness when feeling anger called "Why Mindfulness is a Super Power – an animation".

6. Tackle your thoughts and perspectives. Anger is often fuelled by the ruminative negative (biased) thoughts we talked about earlier. When you are ready, take some time to write down what you are thinking about the situation that is triggering the anger. What are you thinking about yourself, others, your future, your past, your children, your life? Try to write this all down. Then, try to be really honest with yourself and see if there are any biases or inaccuracies in your thinking (see page 47). Are you thinking fairly, rationally, calmly about the situation? Are there other ways to look at it? Could there be other perspectives to keep in mind? Could the other person in the situation have other explanations, perspectives, intentions that you haven't considered?

7. Give yourself time. Time for the anger to become less intense and the feelings underneath the anger to reduce. Time to see the situation with a calmer head. Time to talk to others to gain a fairer or neutral perspective.

8. Think about what you want to say and do. Think about communicating how you feel *underneath* the anger rather than communicating the anger. Think about the style of communication/behaviour you want to use, and whether this is calm and assertive and reasonable. If not, think about whether you need more time to help you get to this place. Think about the consequences of what may happen if you communicate your anger with aggression/passive aggression, or if you communicate based on the angry, biased thinking that may be present. Give yourself time to think all this through.

9. Think about whether it will help to communicate your anger with the person/situation, or whether it would be

better to share it with others/in therapy/work through it yourself. It is important to talk about how we feel, but deciding who, how, where and why to talk can be important too; to make sure it helps your mental health and improves situations. Because anger is such a volatile emotion, it is important to take time to think about where, with whom and how to express it.

10. Remember it is okay to communicate how you feel, but aim to do this by responding calmly, fairly and assertively, rather than reacting angrily, impulsively, aggressively, irrationally. Use "I" statements: "I felt really sad when you did X", "It really hurt me when X happened". This is much better than "you" statements; for example, "You made me feel X", "You did X".

11. Be open to hearing the other person's perspective. Be open to negotiation and compromise and finding a way forward. Be open to not staying angry. Be open to resolving the situation.

12. Be the bigger person. Be the adult. Be the calm one. Be the reasonable one. Be the fair one. Model for your children how you can calmly manage situations that cause hurt and anger.

13. If you do react, own your anger – be accountable. Communicate that you know you reacted in anger and apologize for this.

14. Remember it is okay to let your anger go; you don't always have to react or respond to it. You can just focus on you and how to let it go, or, once you have communicated in a healthy way, you can learn ways to let it go. When we ruminate, stew on our anger, keep it going, provoke it, we only harm ourselves. Holding on to anger is like burning down your own home: it only serves to harm you and those close to you. Every time you

imagine that fire trying to burn, imagine pouring water over it, and moving on.

15. With any difficult situation, you can try to move the focus from how it made you feel (once you have had time to make sense of this and work through this) to what you can learn from this.

OTHER WAYS TO RELEASE, SOOTHE OR CONTAIN YOUR ANGER

- See a couples therapist, counsellor or psychologist.
- Talk to a friend or family member, a neutral person who you can trust to listen, to give you a calm, reasonable view and to be kind.
- Play your favourite music really loud – choose songs that you can sing out loud as expressing anger through the song can be very cathartic.
- Write down your anger – everything you are thinking and feeling. You can write in huge capital letters, red pen, scribbles across the page – whatever you want. When you have finished, you can keep it, rip it up into a hundred pieces, paint over it, and so on. It is not advised to share this type of expressive writing with the person you are angry at, as this rarely helps. This exercise is for you alone.
- Shout or scream into a pillow, or find a spot outdoors where you can scream into the wind.
- If you are by yourself, use the pillow as a punch bag. This isn't a long-term strategy, but can be helpful in the moment as an outlet for the rage.
- Do some physical sport or activity where you can put all your frustrations and tension into the activity.
- Stand facing the wall and, with your arms outstretched, push into the wall; push into your hands/arms and into

your feet. Notice all the feelings in your body and the feeling of pushing out the anger and tension.

- Take a very cold shower, splash your face with ice-cold water or hold ice cubes. This helps to change the physiological response in the body to a calmer state.

General Ways to Reduce the Likelihood of/or Intensity of Anger

- Look after yourself: practise self-care; get some sleep; rest; eat well; monitor your alcohol intake.
- Seek and accept help; don't try to do everything yourself. Your ex-partner or your family might not step up to childcare as much as you might like, so acknowledge this and explore other sources of help.

IF YOUR ANGER COMES OUT AT THE CHILDREN

You may find your anger toward your situation bubbles over in your parenting, or your children are triggers for your anger (particularly if you are a parent to teenagers). All the strategies explored above apply, as your main aim is to focus on staying calm.

If you become angry with your children, try to take yourself out of the situation temporarily; if that isn't possible, stop and employ the crisis management strategies (see page 53) as soon as you can.

Communicate with your child as soon as you are able that you didn't want to get angry around them/toward them, that you are sorry, that you are feeling angry/sad/tired right now and your anger got the better of you.

It is okay to let them know that you are human, that you make mistakes, or struggle with your emotions at times. There is so much value in recognizing this, and being open and honest. Let them know reacting in anger is something you will try hard not to do, and model this to your children to help them be able to do the same. You don't have to share the full details of what may be going on; it is okay to keep some boundaries between the child/parent relationship.

HOW TO CO-PARENT WITHOUT ANGER SETTING IN

Anger within the co-parenting relationship is very common. But finding ways to communicate and co-parent without the anger taking over is going to be so, so, so helpful in the long run, as it will not be good for your mental health to be in constant conflict and a state of anger and rage with your ex-partner. It will also be incredibly detrimental to your children to see their parents fighting, shouting, screaming, arguing. However much you think children are protected from this, they aren't. Children can pick up on the atmosphere, on the hushed unpleasantness, and on the stress and tension and conflict, even without either of you saying a word. And, of course, when they are witness to arguments and anger they are affected – at any age.

So, no matter how your partner interacts with you, aim to do your best to maintain civil, polite, non-antagonistic interactions. This might mean biting your tongue at times; it might mean containing your anger to process with loved ones or elsewhere; it might mean having to step away at times. Do whatever you need to do.

- Respect. Aim to maintain a basic level of respect for each other and, if applicable, their partners. Even though you really may not like it, your ex-partner and co-parent will always be a part of your and your child's life. You are the people your children look to as their parents, and who your children deserve to see treating each other okay, if not for each other's sake then for the sakes of your children. Keeping a level of respect can help in avoiding potential confrontations.

- Discretion. Don't bad mouth your ex-partner or their new partner to your child. No matter how tempting it is, how furious you are, how frustrated you feel – don't do it. No kid wants to hear their parents talking badly of each other; and if your child tells your ex what you've said, it will cause even more friction and potentially spark a chain reaction of unpleasantness with your child stuck in the middle. Try to avoid this at all costs.

THE IMPACT OF WARRING PARENTS

Divorce, separation, relationship breakdowns, or fighting separated parents can all have an impact on children that can be seen into adulthood. Children who experience or witness anger, fighting, conflict, warring parents who won't speak to each other and so on, can go on to experience anxiety, anger issues, trauma, self-esteem issues or low mood in later life. Of course, this is not always and not everyone – but it is enough to know the importance of doing the best to keep things calm, civil, respectful.

You cannot take responsibility for how your co-parent behaves – so please don't feel you have to do this – but you can focus on how you behave and respond, and find ways to do this as calmly and civilly as possible.

- Boundaries. Set clear boundaries with your ex as soon as you are able to start discussing moving forward as co-parents.
- A co-parenting plan. If it is not possible to set this up together, sit down with a neutral person and hash out the details, such as when the child will stay with you and when they will stay with your ex-partner; how you will manage birthdays and Christmases; how you will communicate about important details like school news or illnesses, etc. You can then all stick to this agreement and everyone, including your child (where appropriate), knows what is happening.
- Communication. Agree ways to communicate, whether through text, phone, email, etc. Aim to maintain communication pathways directly between the two of you, rather than via your children, as this is incredibly unhealthy pressure for children, even if they are teenagers or adult children. If the anger and rage mean it is impossible to communicate calmly, see if you can find someone who can act as a neutral mediator. Amy and her ex have a group chat with their son's grandmother, who works as a mediator. She's helped calm down situations in the past as she can see both their points of view and makes sure that their son is always the focus.
- Flexibility. Now we're not saying you should let things slide all the time, but allowing a little bit of flexibility with your ex could be beneficial to you in the long run. For example, by becoming more flexible with pick-ups and drop-offs with their son, Amy's ex has become more flexible too, which gives both parties a bit more freedom.

PSYCHOLOGICAL FLEXIBILITY

Psychological flexibility is a very healthy trait to develop. The more flexible we are, the more we can accommodate challenges, be open to change and roll with difficulties that arise. This doesn't mean being a walkover or not being assertive when needed, it just means working with the concept of "Can I be flexible on this issue?". Anger and rage make us rigid and inflexible, and so challenging ourselves to practise flexibility can be very helpful in getting us out of this rageful place.

WORKING THROUGH THE RAGE

Now we're not condoning pettiness when you're dealing with a Hulk outburst (but definitely not *not* condoning it). After a heated argument, Frenchie, a single mum of three years, was sent some extra money from her ex because she was struggling; she explains, "Like a totally spoilt brat, I spent it on an extortionate swimming costume because, fuck him! I don't even swim. I don't understand. It's so weird being so poor with such an expensive swimming costume. I can't even take it back!" Now, sure, we've all done things we regret out of anger … one mum's moment involved some broken golf clubs, and another's may have involved a toothbrush and a toilet … but we won't go there today!

Although your anger is so very understandable, your priority – when you're ready – is to break down this anger and deal with this in a healthy mature way. You might be set on blaming yourself or others for the break-up or for the situation you find yourself in as a single mother, but eventually you'll realize that you're angry (and underneath that anger you are sad, hurt, let down, worried, and so on) at the whole situation itself. In the moment, it just feels so unfair. However, it is the reality, and you need to offer yourself some time for self-reflection in order to get through this. Once you have had time to reflect on your anger, the root causes of it, the feelings underneath it, and had a chance to talk about this, feel it, process it and move through it, you will be able to move forward without the anger following you so intensely. Therapy will help you do this; self-help materials and exercises or good friends can help too.

IS ALL ANGER VALID?

This is a good question. On the one hand, of course, the general principle is that all emotions are valid, and you feel what you feel and no one has the right to tell you otherwise. On the other hand, anger is driven by a very primitive fight or flight system, which isn't sophisticated enough to look at all the triggers and thoughts behind the anger and calmly filter these to ensure we are basing our anger on valid facts and accurate interpretations.

For example, your ex-partner is due to arrive to pick up the children and she doesn't turn up. You are furious. She's letting you and the children down, being unreliable, disrespectful, doesn't care about you or the children and so on. You find your thoughts on this whizzing round your head, angry, thinking about what you will say to her about this situation. You are tempted to cancel childcare arrangements or to tell the children how useless their other parent is. Half an hour later your ex arrives. She is hugely apologetic, explains that she was stuck in a traffic queue because of an accident and her phone ran out of power and her charger wasn't working to call. Now you have a different version of events. Some of those angry thoughts you had earlier aren't really accurate. You might still have feelings of annoyance that she is not organized enough to charge her phone, but this is a milder anger than the one triggered by your earlier thoughts.

So, while we can be kind to ourselves, and recognize we feel what we feel, it is important to be careful to check that we have understood the situation correctly. We need to be sure that our thoughts are not negatively biased and sending us a skewed version of events, which may be inaccurate, only based on a one-sided perspective, or that we haven't misunderstood something before we can decide how valid our anger may be.

COMBAT ANGER WITH COMPASSION

When my relationship ended, my self-esteem was at an all-time low and I felt unworthy of love or affection. It's so common to turn the anger inwards and blame ourselves. Instead of being angry at myself, I wish I had shown myself compassion. I didn't need to blame myself – what was done was done. I needed to find a way to get myself through the break-up unscathed. By judging myself – my looks and my personality – I only made myself feel worse and worse. **Amy**

Compassion toward ourselves or others is an incredible gift we can give ourselves. Research has shown that people who develop a self-compassionate voice, rather than a self-critical and judgemental voice, are far more likely to successfully achieve their goals and move forward in life in a healthy way. Self-compassion doesn't mean letting yourself off the hook or not holding yourself accountable, it just means being kinder to yourself while you do this. If you are late for the school pick-up, you don't have to beat yourself up. You can be kind to yourself: remind yourself that it was a tough day and you were trying to do too much, or a meeting overran which was out of your control. This doesn't mean you are a terrible person or mother. However, you can also gently encourage yourself to learn from this situation, and acknowledge what you may like to do differently next time to avoid the lateness, if there is a way for this to be in your control. If it is not, you may want to plan back-up care in case this arises again in the future.

The way we talk to ourselves is vital. Not only is it important to talk to yourself compassionately for your own sake, but it's also so important for your child to see you giving yourself time to heal and not beating yourself up about feeling bad. We want our children to grow up with a self-compassionate inner dialogue, so we need to show them that we too can have a self-compassionate inner dialogue. Surely that's enough incentive to give self-compassion a go, even if you feel like you don't deserve it.

Self-compassion is:

- Being kind to yourself
- Not judging yourself
- Not being self-critical
- Being fair to yourself
- Being mindful
- Being accountable and responsible – but kindly, gently and fairly
- Acknowledging you won't be the only one dealing with the struggles you are facing
- Talking and supporting yourself like you would a friend or loved one

When you are angry with yourself, try the following compassionate approach:

1. Notice how you are talking to yourself.
2. Imagine your closest friend is in this situation.

65

3. How would you guide, support, be kind to them, showing empathy and compassion and also helping them move forward?
4. Try to talk to yourself in this same way – being kind, supportive, understanding, patient, fair, reasonable, and gently holding yourself accountable and learning from a situation where needed.
5. Think about the way you talk to yourself. Instead of thinking, "I'm so stupid for being upset about this break-up", rephrase your thoughts to "I am upset about this break-up and that is a healthy and normal reaction to this situation".

Wellbeing Exercises

- Keep a diary. We know not everyone enjoys writing. However, even just jotting down your feelings – what made you feel good and what made you feel bad – each day can help you keep ahead of how you are feeling and make it less likely for anger to boil over unnoticed.
- Try meditation. This has really helped Amy reframe her whole outlook around life. Apps such as Headspace have great guided meditations for a lot of situations, including anger.
- Work it out. After Amy and her ex-partner broke up, she took her anger out on weightlifting, which gave her a sense of herself back. While the gym isn't an option for everyone, even things like punching a pillow, dancing to death metal around the house, or going for a peaceful walk can help.
- Forgive yourself. Anger can often come from second-guessing your choices or feeling like you've failed in some way. Life is the way it is right now. You are doing the best you can. Put the past in the past and be kind to yourself in this present moment.

SEPARATE YOURSELF EMOTIONALLY

There may be certain situations where your ex and co-parent behaves in difficult, aggressive, controlling, or unpleasant ways, often triggering your anger, despite any attempts you put in place for civil, respectful and amicable relations. When you have tried to establish healthy, calm communication and it is not working, you may need to try other ways to manage the situation. Amy, for example, tried the "Grey Rock Method".

The Grey Rock Method tends to be used as a coping tool when dealing with narcissists. The premise is that you become uninteresting and unresponsive – basically, you act as dull as a grey rock – when you're communicating with that person. It ultimately stops you feeding the drama and negative attention, and it can be a useful way to calm yourself out of a potentially fiery argument. You might want to try it if conversations with your ex tend to get fiery, or as a way to set boundaries. So, when talking to your ex, you should try to:

1. Not tell them you're practising the Grey Rock Method.
2. Limit your interactions. Only discuss child-related issues and keep communications brief. If the conversation starts going anywhere else, respond blandly.
3. Keep to the facts. Don't give any personal opinions or unnecessary information.
4. Try to distract yourself from any heightened emotions that might arise by thinking about something completely different – such as focusing on your breathing or the clouds moving, anything that can take your mind off the triggers in the conversation.
5. Be private. They do not need to know anything about your life right now, only that of your child. You might choose to delete them from social media so as to limit their access to any additional information about you.

Let It Go

Decide to let an angry issue go rather than letting it hold any power over you, over how you think, feel, behave anymore. Try this today – not for anyone else, but for you, for your wellbeing and your mental health.

Example: Jemma noticed how she was annoyed when her ex-partner didn't help out in a small way she wanted him to with the children. To begin with she was stewing over this and typed out an annoyed message to her ex. Then she took some time – she stepped away. She asked herself, "Is this really worth it?" Then she let it go. She deleted the text, and got on with her day. And she felt much lighter for letting it go.

1. Take some time to think about any current issues causing you anger in your life now.
2. Ask yourself what is it costing you to hold on to this anger? Is it working for you to be angry/stay angry? Does it help you, your children, your situation?
3. Consider what would happen if you just chose to let the anger go. Not to carry it anymore. To know you have the power to let it go if you choose.
4. Consider how it would feel if you let the anger go. If you didn't have to dwell on it, bother with it, ruminate on it, respond to it anymore. Talk to yourself kindly. It's not worth it to hang on to this.
5. Choose to let it go. Imagine the anger in a balloon drifting away. Imagine the thoughts passing by. Imagine as you take a breath you breathe out all the tension and stress. Shake it off. Shrug your arms, roll your shoulders back, shake it all out.
6. You have the power to let it go and be free of it. Move forward. Let it go.

3

SHAME

In a world rife with stereotypes and unhelpful narratives about ourselves, this chapter focuses on the shame around being a single mum. We unpick the stereotype, look at how the social narrative has contributed to single mothers feeling ashamed, hear about experiences of shame in single motherhood, and look at ways to help you overcome these feelings of shame.

If you're sometimes feeling shame about being a single mum, we're right there with you. Not because being a single mum is shameful (it absolutely isn't), but because it has been indoctrinated into us throughout our whole lives. From the media to the people around us, being a single mum has largely been portrayed as a negative experience and the result of poor life choices, mistakes and failures.

In the words of the UK-based single-parent charity Gingerbread, "In 1987, The Family Law Reform Act was introduced, which gave the same legal rights to children born outside of marriage as those born within marriage. It's hard to believe that, until 1987, stigmatisation of single parent families was part of this country's legislation."

SHAMED FROM UP HIGH

In 1994, Rick Santorum, an American politician and former member of the United States Senate, made single mothers a focus of his welfare policy. He tried to introduce a policy that would stop women from applying for welfare if they didn't name their child's father, alongside a bunch of other ludicrous demands. Luckily, this didn't pass the US Congress, but it's clear what Santorum's views of single mothers were: "What we have is moms raising children in single-parent households simply breeding more criminals." This is an outrageously insulting view from a white man in power, blaming single parents for high crime rates, rather than a broken society that benefits the wealthy and scrutinizes the poor. Angry yet? Yep, we are too. But that's not all – UK politicians have been just as bad.

In 1995, current UK Prime Minister Boris Johnson wrote a column for *The Spectator* magazine in which he called single mothers "ill-raised, ignorant, aggressive and illegitimate", before saying that it is "outrageous that married couples should pay for the single mother's desire to procreate independently of men". The fact that this man could pen such abhorrent views, yet still end up as the Prime Minister of Great Britain, tells us that we still have lots of work to do.

In October 1998, former UK Prime Minister Margaret Thatcher told an audience in Kentucky, "We wanted to do our best for them (single mothers), and our best was to see that the young mother had a flat of her own, in the town where she lived and also an income to look after that child ... In tackling the situation that way, we were unwittingly multiplying the number of people who had illegitimate children. Now we think it's better to put these children in the hands of a very good religious order, and the mother as well, so that they too will be brought up with family values." As recently as 1998, a woman with immense political influence was telling the world that single mothers are incapable of looking after themselves, let alone their children. It's this public shaming that has helped instil negative views into us.

Thankfully, many charities such as Gingerbread and the National Council for One Parent Families in the UK and Single Parent Project in the US work tirelessly to fight the stigma against single mothers and ensure support for single-parent households. However, despite the work being put in, we know people still experience a lot of shame surrounding single motherhood.

WHAT IS SHAME?

Shame is a powerful and self-critical emotion. It is one of the most challenging of the emotions because, by its nature, it makes people feel ashamed to even talk about it. Shame itself makes us feel uncomfortable and distressed, as it focuses on the idea that we have done something terrible *and* that we ourselves are terrible. It is a critical self-judgement on ourselves.

Clinical Psychologist Professor Paul Gilbert's excellent work helps us understand shame and self-compassion; in his book *The Compassionate Mind* he wrote:

"When we feel shame, our attention is on ourselves and how others might see us – i.e. think badly of us. In shame, we feel exposed, and think there's something wrong or flawed about us. We feel anxious, depressed and our hearts sink. We put our heads down and avoid the gaze of others, covering up the things we feel ashamed about. If we become shameful to ourselves we do this by being self-critical and contemptuous of ourselves. Shame is, therefore, about threats and attacks and how bad or inadequate we feel we are; it's about judging and being judged."

Dr Brené Brown, an American scholar, author, researcher and public speaker, has spoken and described shame in the following ways:

- Shame is the intensely painful feeling or experience of believing we are flawed and therefore unworthy of acceptance and belonging.
- Women often experience shame when they are entangled in a web of layered, conflicting and competing social-community expectations.
- Shame leaves women feeling trapped, powerless and isolated.
- Shame creates feelings of fear, blame and disconnection.
- Shame, if left to its own devices, can destroy lives.
- The less you talk about it, the more you have got it. Shame needs three things to grow: secrecy, silence and judgement.

WHEN DO PEOPLE EXPERIENCE SHAME AS A SINGLE MOTHER?

People can experience shame through the reactions and responses of friends and family; they can experience shame by self-shaming themselves; and they can experience shame through interactions with people they have never even met.

Shame can arise in the following ways (not an exhaustive list):

- How you feel about being a single-parent family
- How you feel about the fact that your relationship, engagement, marriage or civil partnership has broken down; or how you feel about not being successful in keeping it going

- How you feel about being the person that left, or had an affair
- How you feel about being cheated on
- When you struggle with tasks as a single parent
- When your children ask you why you and your ex-partner aren't together
- When it is suggested you didn't try hard enough at your relationship or you have let your children down
- Having to seek benefit support as a single parent
- Having to seek support from friends or family because you can't manage alone
- When you have not followed social, religious or cultural expectations of your family or community
- When you think you have behaved badly or coped badly in the break-up, maybe reacting in distress or anger

STORIES OF SHAME IN SOLO MOTHERHOOD

Everyone will have different experiences of shame in single parenthood. We share some stories and experiences from incredible single mums here. As you read these, remember to keep in mind, our shame comes from this social narrative that has been constructed through the years, whether that has come from government and political agendas, or from socially acceptable ideals, or cultural or religious norms. As set out at the start of the chapter, when we grow up in an environment that holds implicit ideas about how things should be – for example, if the message is you should be a two-parent, heterosexual, married family – it is easy for shame to grow when you don't fit those expectations. To add to this, the sense of failure and the implication that you haven't succeeded or worked hard enough to keep your relationship together, or that there must be something wrong with you in some way to end up a single parent, or that what you offer as a single parent can't be as good as a two-parent household, all adds to the shame that can be felt.

SHAME FELT FROM FRIENDS AND FAMILY

There are moments in the journey into and along the road of single motherhood that family and friends may respond in ways that make you feel shame. This can be really painful, as this only reinforces any negative feelings you may already be struggling with, and it can be especially hurtful coming from the people you hoped would love and support you. The expectations placed on parents or mothers by the culture you are brought up in or your religion can play a big part in any shame you may feel. If the general expectation is that a successful "family" means a two-parent household then you may end up feeling ashamed if the message is you have "failed" by not maintaining this. If the general expectation is that you do not get divorced, then you may be shamed for going through this process.

> When **Ali's** marriage was breaking down, and she and her partner had exhausted couple's therapy, she felt ashamed to tell her family. "My husband and I were both so unhappy together, there seemed to be nothing we could do to make it work and it was starting to affect the children. We both wanted a divorce, but I was so scared of what my family and other people in our society would think – we come from a religious background and divorce is not looked upon lightly. I was lucky that when I did buck up the courage to tell my mother, she reacted perfectly. However, I do feel like a lot of other people are talking behind my back because of it."

Sometimes this shaming can be quite overt, and you find yourself having to respond to other people's narrowminded opinions on the single mum stereotype.

> When **Arabella** unexpectedly became pregnant at 18, she faced stigma from family and friends.
> "When I first fell pregnant, I announced it to family and friends at the pub. A family friend came over and said, 'I hope you don't turn into one of those council estate mums on benefits.'"

There's a hyper-stereotyping of single mums who receive support from the government. Firstly, there is absolutely nothing wrong with living in social housing, and anyone that thinks there *is* must be extremely privileged. Secondly, the benefits system is there to support people who need it, which includes single mothers who can struggle to be able to work due to their parenting responsibilities, or to find affordable childcare.

> **Arabella's** grandparents also took the news of her pregnancy really badly.
> "I was supposed to be their first grandchild going to university. My nan didn't speak to me until my son was born. She never asked me how I was or how I was getting on. It took a while before she accepted it and a long time for us to rebuild our relationship."

Sometimes the shaming message can be more subtle. Even when family members or friends are trying to be supportive, there can be an underlying feeling of shame, whether it's their intention or not.

> **Ellie's** parents have been supportive of her relationship breakdown. However, she's noticed that they always

drop into conversation when someone else is a single mum or divorced.

"I'm sure it is with the intention to reassure me that it happens to a lot of people, but it feels like a constant reminder of this new identity that I have, not only in my eyes but in everyone else's too."

Jemma *also found these subtle messages creeping into her conversations with her family.*

"When I told my family I was separating, they sent me messages asking if I had really thought about the impact on my children as it was going to be really damaging. I felt terrible, because there was so much implied in these messages, that made me feel shame. Of course I had considered my children, and of course I wasn't taking this decision lightly, and of course I was terrified about the impact on them; but actually I knew what would be more damaging for them: being in a situation with incredibly unhappy parents."

SELF-SHAMING

Often, we'll put the shame on ourselves. We'll feel embarrassed that we ended up in this situation, and not want to publicize that we are single mums or that we are divorced. Many of us have grown up thinking the ideal situation to be in when you're older is married with kids ... not *alone* with kids. If you have your own beliefs or values about staying in a relationship/marriage with a child, about separation or divorce, about being a single-parent family, or about fidelity – if you feel you acted against your own beliefs or values – this can bring feelings of shame. For example, if you have core values of honesty, trust, kindness or self-control and your behaviour hasn't shown this (perhaps as your relationship broke down you became unkind, mean, argumentative, not fully truthful, in response to the situation), then you may end up experiencing shame for how your behaviour has conflicted with these core values.

Ellie *felt a lot of shame from herself.*

"I always wanted to be married before I had children so that we would share the same surname and because I wanted to raise my family in a 'stable environment' (oh the irony!). When it became apparent that my marriage was ending and that I was essentially now a single mum, I struggled with accepting this new identity. I always had an ideal life planned in my head, and being a single mum was far from it."

Frenchie *is a young single mum, and she thinks most of the shame she felt came from herself.*

"I felt so ashamed about being a young single mum that I became obsessed with proving that I could be a 'good mum' (as if there was some implication or fear that everyone would think that as a young single mum then I would be a bad mum). I rigidly stuck to weird and strict rules of parenting because I thought it would give me credentials among the older women at baby groups or sat nearby at Costa. However, I started going to local meet-ups with a diverse mix of families from a Facebook group. Sitting in the park and talking about how difficult parenting was, and how annoying our kids could be, definitely started to take the edge off, and then I could let my rigid rules relax a bit. And now I don't care about others' opinions or the little shitty internal voice that sometimes pops back up."

Bella *noted she tended to get caught up in self-shaming when she had to do solo events, like parents' evenings, sports days for the first time, or when she was out with the children on her own.*

77

"I would feel so shamed about being on my own, I felt like people were judging me, and staring at me."

Katie *also felt a sense of shame when she thought about her children not growing up in a two-parent household.*

"Every morning for a long time after I became a single parent, I would wake up and it would hit me all over again. I was a single parent. My children were growing up in a household without two parents. I felt like such a failure. I had failed my children. I hadn't tried hard enough. It was a terrible feeling."

SHAME FROM STRANGERS

Let's talk about being shamed by random strangers. We would all love to be that person who doesn't care what strangers think of them, but for most of us there is always that little niggling feeling that we don't want people thinking negatively of us or our family situation. The problem with strangers is they don't know anything about your life, and could never possibly know that you might be in a better place now.

Romy *has found that when people find out she is not married they feel sorry for her because things didn't work out with her son's father.*

"I am not sorry about such things because he really is a manipulative, violent person, and I am proud that I got away."

Sometimes people are a bit more obvious with their single-mum shaming, especially when it comes to dating. Allison and Frankie have both dealt with potential dates showing their true colours early. Allison was told that the man she was interested in, "Only dates single mums because we're easy." Wow! While Frankie dated a man who thought the only reason she wanted to date was because she was desperate for a man for security. Yes, because obviously all we want in life is your passé patriarchal opinions and your hard-earned cash – could we eyeroll any harder? We explore the world of dating further on in the book, and we promise it's not all bad!

> **Cleo** *took her daughter on holiday to a caravan park and spent the evening at the entertainment bar.*
>
> *"I was sat alone as she was playing with other kids and a lady came over to borrow a chair. She asked if anyone was joining me and I said no. She responded with, 'Oh right, I'm here with my family, I wouldn't expect to see someone on their own.' It made me feel so uncomfortable because, well, I'm a single mum, I didn't choose to be there on my own but, hey, that's life!"*

Unfortunately, some people just might not think about their choice of words, and you need to not let them get to you. It's hard, but you can learn to just shake it off. These people don't know you, may just be being careless in their words, and ultimately don't deserve to have too much power over you and how you feel. It's something you can work on, and something that will benefit you greatly in the long run, with numerous situations!

While we're doing our best to pick apart a deeply set cultural view that single motherhood is something to be ashamed of, the most important thing to think about is how *you* feel about your situation. We are not going to change the world's view instantly, but what we can do is change the way we feel about ourselves.

HOW TO RISE ABOVE STRANGERS' OPINIONS

- Remind yourself that these people are not worth your time; their words may have upset you or made you uncomfortable, but whatever they have said is on them and has nothing to do with you.
- Think about things that make you happy, and remind yourself how awesome a job you are doing.
- Focus on the positive comments you've received since becoming a single mum.

OVERCOMING SHAME AND COMING THROUGH STRONGER

Owning our own story and loving ourselves through that process is the bravest thing we will ever do.

Brené Brown, *The Gifts of Imperfection*

PRACTICAL TIPS ON OVERCOMING SHAME

- Stand tall and celebrate yourself! You're a boss and don't let anyone tell you you're not.
- Be kind to yourself. You're a human being, deserving of kindness, affection and joy.
- Surround yourself with like-minded people – it is such a great way to combat the self-shaming attitude we so often have.
- Don't pressure yourself into being the "perfect" mum. Spend time with other mums and learn to be content with the real you!

- Think about all the positive things you've done since becoming a single parent.
- Don't compare yourself to who you were before the relationship breakdown.
- Remember that becoming a single mum means a new identify, but also that our identities will constantly be changing and that is okay.
- Give yourself time for *you* – self-care can do wonders.
- Think about what goals you'd like to achieve in the next few years and focus on them.
- Talk to your friends or find some support groups for single parents and make new friends – the Frolo app is fantastic for this.

PSYCHOLOGICAL WAYS TO OVERCOME SHAME

Start with the important premise that *you do not have to hold on to shame in your life*. You *do not deserve to hold on to shame in your life*. No matter what. Shame holds no purpose but to make us feel bad. You can choose to release shame and let shame go.

Whether it is shame that comes from yourself or from others, you can do the following:

- Notice the shame when it shows up.
- Acknowledge what has triggered the shame.
- Notice how it feels and if/where you feel this in your body.
- Compassionately and firmly remind yourself you do not deserve to hold on to shame in your life.
- If needed, be kind to yourself, be compassionate to yourself, forgive yourself, in relation to whatever has triggered this shame.
- If needed you can learn from the situation that has triggered the shame and make a note for how you want to be if future scenarios arise.

- Notice if you are pulled toward unhelpful behaviours when you feel shame (e.g. drugs, alcohol, bingeing, cigarettes). You might be pulled toward unhelpful strategies of avoidance or withdrawal. You might be pulled toward self-criticism, self-hatred, self-rage. If this happens, change the behaviours. If you are withdrawing, try to do the opposite. Instead of reaching for a drink, go out for a walk, journal, reach out to a friend. Seek help if you need to.

Try practising compassionate self-talk:
- "I am doing my best."
- "There is no shame in being a single parent who is doing the best for themself and their children. There is strength and resilience and bravery."
- "I am where I am. No one is defined by one experience or relationship. I am greater than any one part of my experience. I am proud of myself for getting through this."
- If you feel you have made a mistake, own this but with kindness: "I made a mistake. I am allowed to be forgiven; I am not perfect, no human is."

Rewrite the narrative of single motherhood for yourself. For example:
- "I am a single mother. Being a single mum means I can do X, Y, Z."
- "It means I draw on my strengths, which include ... (e.g. commitment, decision-making, communicating, etc)."
- "It means I learn these new skills, such as ... (e.g. DIY, cooking, swimming, etc)."
- "It means I will find the freedom to choose (insert food, hobbies, TV shows, etc)."

- "It does not define me – I am also … (list other important things about you and your life: a friend, an auntie, a yoga teacher, a runner, a history-lover, etc)."

Now let that shame go. You might physically give it a little shake to release it. You might wrap yourself up in kindness and compassion. You can say to the shame, you can pass now. It might drift away or hang around. Practise noticing it but not being consumed/believing in it.

Try the kind hands exercise (below) to send yourself love and compassion.

Kind Hands

1. When you feel shame, notice where you feel this in your body.
2. Place a hand on wherever you feel the shame.
3. Imagine your hand is holding all the kind acts you have done in your life – cradled your baby, hugged a friend, stroked a pet, helped a neighbour, etc.
4. Imagine sending all that warmth and kindness to yourself right now.
5. Feel the warmth from your hand radiating through to your skin, into your body, to where you are feeling the shame, the pain, the hurt.
6. Send yourself this love and kindness and warmth.
7. Just breathe and allow this warmth to flow round you.

Adapted from Dr Russ Harris.

As shame grows through secrecy, silence and self-judgement, one of the most effective ways to overcome shame is to talk about this with someone who can offer empathy, understanding and support. While there may be some friends or family who have made comments that have brought you shame, there will be others who are enlightened enough to bring you support and kindness. Trust in the people who you know can offer this. Be brave in sharing how you feel. You deserve this support. Don't let shame grow in silence. Talk to a therapist if you feel you cannot talk to friends or family or you are struggling to let the shame go.

PHYSICAL WAYS TO OVERCOME SHAME

Hold your head up high – literally. Shame makes us physically shrink and withdraw into ourselves. Combat this by changing your body posture. Hold your head high. Move your shoulders back. Look people in the eye. Research shows when we change our body posture it can change our mood and how we are thinking. Imagine yourself standing tall like a lion, proud and strong. Even if you don't feel proud and strong, when we act as if we are, drawing on the strength we may need from this, it can change how we feel.

Use this approach when you have to walk into a difficult situation where you know shame may show up. You can choose whatever image or metaphor you like to imagine feeling strong and brave and powerful (imagine walking like a lion, strong and proud into the room).

A Practical and Reflective Exercise for Overcoming Your Experience of Shame

This reflective practice has been taken/adapted from ACT pioneer Dr Russ Harris.

1. If shame were no longer an issue for you:
- What would you stop doing or start doing, or do more of or less of?
- How would you treat yourself, others, life, the world differently?
- What goals would you pursue?
- What activities would you start or resume?
- What people, places, events, activities, challenges would you approach, start, resume or contact – rather than avoid or withdraw from?

2. Once you have answered these questions, take a moment to think about the answers you have given and ask yourself:
- Can I start working toward these now?
- Can I be kind and empathic and self-compassionate to myself and allow myself to take steps toward this life that I have described?
- Can I let myself know that it is okay to do this, and that I won't let allow shame to overcome me and stop me?

Source: Working with Shame: Practical tips for ACT therapists. Dr Russ Harris. 2017. www.imlearningact.com

4

GUILT

The big "G" loves to get involved in parenting, from guilt over leaving your baby for the first time to guilt when they fall off the sofa on your watch. And it doesn't get any more comfortable when you become a single parent. You might feel guilty for any number of reasons – because you're the one who ended the relationship, because your child has to split their time between two parents, or because you feel like you could have done things differently. Perhaps your guilt stems from relying on the support of family or friends. Guilt is a horrible feeling, and can be accompanied by shame, anxiety and anger.

WHAT IS GUILT?

Guilt is an emotion we experience when we believe we have done something wrong. Guilt can be triggered by doing something we perceive as "bad" or "wrong", but it can also be triggered if we think we have failed to do something or if we have hurt or harmed someone else. Guilt often involves blaming ourselves, holding ourselves responsible, or being self-critical or judgemental. It is closely linked to shame. However, we can distinguish these emotions in simple terms, as shame tends to be more pervasive with a focus on "I *am* bad", whereas guilt tends to be more specific to certain events or behaviours with a focus on "I *did* something bad".

Guilt can come about because of one of two factors:

1. We *have* (objectively) made a mistake or intentionally behaved in a way that society on the whole would say is legally, ethically or morally "wrong" (although please note this concept of what society deems wrong is socially constructed and can change over time), and we now hold ourselves responsible and feel guilty for this behaviour. For example, in most cultures infidelity is generally viewed as an unacceptable behaviour in society, and someone committing infidelity may feel guilty for this behaviour or the impact of this behaviour.

2. We *believe* (perspective) that we have done something wrong or failed at something, and we perceive ourselves to be at fault and therefore feel guilty (this is about our *perception* of wrongdoing rather than an *objective truth* of wrongdoing). For example, "I feel guilty because I have failed to keep my marriage together" is a belief or perspective of the situation, but in reality there are likely more complex factors at play that have impacted on the outcome of the marriage; the reality is this is an interaction between two people and both have a responsibility to contribute to making the marriage work, and in some circumstances no matter how hard you try you cannot save the situation.

WHAT DOES GUILT FEEL LIKE?

To put it bluntly, feeling guilty is shit. Similar to shame, guilt can be an incredibly difficult emotion to experience; it can be completely debilitating, and sometimes you might feel like it's swallowing you up or taking over your life. Even if in your heart of hearts you know what has happened is the best option for your family, it doesn't make it any easier to deal with this feeling.

Guilt can make you feel on edge, irritable or anxious; it can also cause physical symptoms such as headaches, insomnia and stomach problems. If your issues with guilt become chronic, it is possible you'll develop other mental health problems, such as anxiety or depression (see later chapters). Unfortunately, as with all emotions there's not a magic cure for guilt; however, there are ways we can deal with guilt to stop it from taking over our lives.

My main source of guilt used to be the thought of my child not having two parents in a loving relationship. It would make me sad, and I'd suffer with insomnia. As time has progressed, I've learnt to deal with this guilt by dissecting why I feel guilty that I can't provide a two-parent household for my child. Over time (and it often takes time), I've come to terms with the fact his dad and I are no longer in a relationship, so can't provide him with that two-adult household together. My guilt stemmed from what I thought was best for my son. As I was feeling guilty because I believed he should be in a two-parent household, I needed to analyse why I believed that set-up would be the best option for him and look at the reality of the situation, which was we were not in a good relationship and if we had continued that could have caused more issues for all of us in the long run. His dad is able to provide a two-parent household for him with his current girlfriend, and one day I might do the same; but at the moment, a one-parent household feels perfect for us right now. **Amy**

STORIES OF GUILT IN SINGLE MOTHERHOOD

Below is a list of common experiences of guilt in single motherhood; however, while these are common situations about which people express *feeling* guilty, this *does not mean* these are reasons you *should* feel guilty.

- When you have to tell your children about the separation
- When you are not providing your child/children a two-parent household/typical "family"
- When you are not able to do two-parent/family activities, holidays, Christmas
- Because you left the relationship
- Because you think you didn't try hard enough to save the relationship
- Because you blame yourself in some way for your situation
- Because you think you didn't "choose well" with your child's parent
- Because you aren't coping
- Because you worry about the impact of a family relationship breakdown on the children
- Because you are tired or snappy with the children
- Because you feel like you don't do enough with the children (play time, bedtime stories, positive attention, school work, hobbies)
- Because you feel snappy with friends when they may not understand the single-parent pressures
- Because you can't attend events for the children; for example, school events because of your work commitments
- If your child is bullied for being in a single-parent family

- Because you can't provide for your children financially in the same way as you did when there was a two-parent income
- Because you have to rely on others for help, support or finances
- When you go out and do things for you, or put yourself first
- For not enjoying your "time off" or finding it difficult

GUILT FROM THINGS THE CHILDREN SAY

With such a big change in your family dynamic, your child is bound to have some tough questions for you. They might also say or comment on things innocently that instantly hits you with immense guilt and sadness. If they're young they won't understand the complexity of adult relationships, and all they're seeing is their parents not being together anymore. What they have gotten so used to over the years is suddenly changing, and it's scary or confusing for them so they might ask questions or talk about it to try to understand what they are seeing and experiencing. These questions or statements will be their way of expressing how they are feeling – *this is rarely your child trying to make you feel guilty*. However, it's easy to end up feeling really guilty.

> **Tegan** *has very recently been through a break-up.*
> *"Nothing breaks my heart more than seeing the tears in his eyes as he tells me he misses daddy when he is here and me when he is there. I hate the idea of breaking his world in two, and that I have ripped his world apart."*

Tegan's guilt is almost tangible – and understandable to some degree. Her child's feelings of sadness and loss are, of course, valid and real – but this is separate from Tegan's feelings of guilt which are projected onto the situation. Tegan does not need to take the emotional burden of guilt on. However, the only way to stop taking on this guilt may be difficult, but *is* necessary – you need to be able to *sit* with your child's thoughts and hurt without turning those words into feelings of guilt. We'll talk about how to do this later in this chapter.

> **Katie** *felt guilt when her children would talk about the separation or about what they miss.*
>
> *"My children would say things like 'Why aren't you and daddy together anymore', or 'I miss my old bedroom, it was so much bigger'. At one time my eldest drew a heart on the shower in steam with mummy and daddy written inside it. He wasn't a big talker, and sometimes my guilt came from what he didn't say. I was constantly worried about what he wasn't saying about the separation but might be thinking in his head, and I would then feel guilty about that."*

There might be times where it seems like your child tries to make you feel guilty on purpose. While we cannot speak for every situation and every child, it can be helpful to keep in mind that while it may feel this way, it might not be exactly what is going on. It is possible for a child to be angry, hurt, scared and more during the transition from a two-parent family to a single-parent family. Depending on their age and understanding, they may be going through their own grief and loss process, at their developmental level, which may mean they have limited understanding of the situation or the emotions coming up for them. Also, as part of this they may lash out in anger and hurt and say things that make you feel terribly guilty. However, this might not really be their intention, they may just be really hurting and you are their safe place to lash out to.

However, statements such as "It's your fault. It's your fault daddy left because you weren't nice to him", or "Mummy says you have a new girlfriend and that's why mummy can't be here", or any variation on this can be really upsetting to hear. These may be exacerbated if the relationship has broken down with your ex-partner to the point where it is not amicable or civil and you or your ex-partner may have shared unkind statements about the other with your child, or infidelity may have been disclosed, and so on. Or perhaps your child has overhead something during a row and either put two and two together or misunderstood what they have heard.

Whatever the situation, and even if your child may be trying to make you feel guilty (remember this requires more developmental skill and understanding than most younger children will be able to do), try to hold in mind your child must be hurting right now to lash out. Try to make space and time to sit with them, listen to and validate their emotions and their thoughts, and give them space and time to talk about and process how they feel.

Dealing with Tricky Questions

Children are unpredictable and can occasionally ask difficult questions, such as why two parents can't get back together. Those questions can hit you out of the blue, but here are some ways to respond to them.

- Q: Mummy, why can't you and Daddy live together again?
  A: Mummy and Daddy lived together because we were in a relationship, but we aren't anymore, and so we live in different houses now.
- Q: Why did you and daddy break up?
  A: Daddy and I decided that we didn't want to be in a relationship anymore. Sometimes people decide that it is better to be friends, or that they make each

other a bit sad and grumpy and so it is better to be separate instead.

- Q: Do you think you and Daddy will ever be together again?
  A: No, I'm sorry we won't be.
- Q: I want you and Daddy to get back together.
  A: I'm afraid that wouldn't work for us, but I understand you might want that. Do you want to talk about it? (Listen, be empathic and supportive.)

GUILT FROM THE IMPACT ON THE CHILDREN

It is common to experience guilt when you think about how the separation and single-parent life may impact your children. You might feel this whether the children seem okay or not.

Jemma explains how she would think about how the separation would change her children's lives, and this made her feel terribly guilty.

"I would worry (and then feel so guilty) about whether they would be psychologically affected by growing up in a single-parent household, by seeing their dad less frequently, or by having to navigate having two houses or step-families and so on. I would think about how it would affect their ability to have a relationship in their future. I would think about the fact they had to deal with this in the first place and blame myself. I would notice all these thoughts and feelings coming up when we had social events and they were the only child without two parents there. And, to be honest, I had all these thoughts and feelings even though my children seemed to cope really well!"

GUILT FROM SEEING TWO-PARENT HOUSEHOLDS

As young kids grow up and see more and more two-parent households they might be sad or confused as to why they don't have that, and it could cause upset which can lead you to feel guilty. You might also feel guilty yourself when you see two-parent households and it reminds you of what your child no longer has.

> **Arabella** feels guilty when her and her son see families together.
> "Often, I'm the only mum at my son's football sessions, and at one match he asked me why I always have to be the only parent at the side-lines while everyone else has their dads there."

While Arabella doesn't deserve to feel the guilt from this, it's her natural reaction when her son is upset about something and she can't find a way of fixing it or making him feel better.

GUILT FOR HAVING "TIME OFF"
As well as the guilt that can show up when your child has to go to the other parent's house or navigate two households, there is also the guilt related to the "time off" you suddenly have.

There can be guilt that you only have this time off in the first place because of the separation, and there can be guilt about whether you are using the time wisely, or enjoying it or appreciating it enough, or even that other mums you know with two-parent households might not have this time off and so you feel guilty for complaining about having this time when they don't!

It is important to remember that this isn't "time off" any more than being on maternity leave is "having a holiday". It is what it is, time without your children while they spend time with their other parent because you are now separated; it isn't a lovely bit of time off that you have asked for, although you can with time learn to love it and appreciate it.

Ellie *struggles when her child stays at her dad's.*

"Friends who aren't single parents make comments about me getting time off every week, which makes me feel guilty for not enjoying it, but for me that time off is time where my child is going to play happy families with her dad and someone who isn't her mum. I didn't choose to be a part-time mum or share my child with a step-mum. In fact, I sleep much worse when she is away from home than when she is with me!"

While feeling guilty that your child spends time at a different house is normal, it's also cutting into your time of looking after yourself and doing things for you. Ideally, this time would be spent giving yourself that much-needed break – a reset for your mind and body.

Katie described:

"I started off hating my 'time off' when the children were at their other household. I felt guilty for not enjoying it properly, and guilty my children had to separate their weekends in different homes. Over time, I got used to that and began to be good at making plans and using the time for me. But then I found myself feeling guilty when an event for the children would come up on my 'time off' when I had plans, so would have the conflict of deciding whether to cancel my plans or keep them, knowing they have their other parent there, and that is okay. I knew rationally it was okay not to cancel, but I would also feel really guilty if I actioned this."

GUILT FOR THE JUGGLING ACT
Then there's the age-old struggle of juggling your time with different people. Especially if you start up a new relationship with someone. We're often trying to balance so many different

plates at once, such as parenting, working, cleaning, socializing and maybe even dating. Sometimes it can all get too much, and it makes us feel overwhelmed.

> When **Allison** got into a relationship, she often felt like she was letting someone down.
> "When I was with Esme, my then girlfriend, I would feel like I was constantly torn between my relationship with her and my kids. It felt like I couldn't give my all to both of them. If I was spending too much time with Esme, I was doing the kids a disservice, and if I was spending lots of time with the kids, Esme would complain that I was not paying her attention."

Feeling the struggle between balancing your relationship with your partner and your kids links to feelings of guilt and that you're always letting somebody down. You should never be made to feel like you have to choose between your children and someone else; if this is happening, then you need to rethink the people you're spending your time with and work out whether these are worthwhile relationships to be keeping.

GUILT FOR CHOOSING THE WRONG PERSON TO SPEND A LIFE WITH

Your guilt might have stemmed from your own decisions. If you were in a bad relationship, you could be feeling guilty for choosing that person to start a family with. Unfortunately, we are really good at putting the blame on ourselves! Of course, you are responsible for your own actions, but in no way are you responsible for how someone else acts. If you entered into a relationship with someone who turned out to behave badly, you didn't choose for them to treat you badly, you didn't choose for them to manipulate you, you didn't choose unhappiness, and you aren't responsible for their behaviours. What you did choose was to get out of that relationship. Whether you managed to get out quickly or you feel like you stayed for too long (in hindsight), should not affect how you feel about yourself, because, guess what? You've done it! Well done!

Kelly *was in an abusive relationship, and although she struggles with guilt, it's not because she is now a single mum but it's because she feels like she spent too long in that relationship.*

"I feel guilty that I picked a bad man to spend so much of my life with, and that I didn't take the red flags seriously or stand up for myself. Some of the moments when I should have had more faith in myself – or stood my ground – still haunt me, especially on low days or if my self-esteem has taken a bit of a bashing."

GUILT FOR NOT HAVING ANOTHER CHILD

Another reason for feeling guilty might be because you aren't in a position to give your child a sibling. While we have touched upon this subject in the Grief chapter, it's also very relevant here. Life rarely turns out how we plan – not many of us expected to become single mums when we were younger! You might feel unhappy that your child will always be an only child or that in any future family dynamics your child will always have a separate family that they go away to.

Frenchie *shares these feelings.*
"I hate that he's an only child, and the thought that if I were to introduce more in the future he would be between

houses and the other one wouldn't. There's a lot of guilt, but I try to push it down because life would have been much worse if I stayed with my ex."

Frenchie being able to put her guilt into perspective and realize that her life is much better out of that relationship is helping her to move forward. By thinking about what makes us feel guilty and why, we can start working through the guilt. However, it would be great for Frenchie not to push down her guilt, or *any* emotions, but instead find ways to process it and let it go instead.

> **Cleo's** biggest guilt is not being able to give her daughter a sibling.
> *"I never wanted an only child, but now at 43 and single it's just never going to happen. I so wish I could have done things slightly different (like be in a happy relationship) and had more children."*

GUILT FOR RELYING ON SUPPORT

Whatever circumstances led to you becoming a single mum, it can be hard for us to ask for support. You might feel like your child is your responsibility and no one else should feel like they need to help.

> **Arabella**, pregnant at 18 and not in a relationship with the father, needed support from the moment her son was born.
> *"When he was first born, I felt so guilty asking my mum or sister to babysit. I felt so guilty, I couldn't even enjoy that alone time."*

While Arabella felt like she shouldn't have to ask other people to help, her family were all willing and delighted to be able to.

GUILT FOR NEEDING TO WORK

Whether it's for career or financial purposes, or you just need some time to yourself, to do the things that make you feel like you, we still manage to make ourselves feel guilty! While it would be great to be able to spend loads of time with our children, we've got to earn money to provide. Feeling guilty because we need to go out to work is very counter-intuitive for our mental health. Things can be tight when you go from being a two-parent household to just one, you might have had to take up more work or use the benefit system. But whatever we do, we are still going to feel guilty about it!

Romy works full time as a senior physiotherapist in a busy intensive care unit.

"I worked throughout lockdown, I work on-call shifts overnight and I work long weeks. I rely solely on my parents for childcare outside of school hours, and I feel terrible if I miss something school-related or can't do lots of fun activities with him. I feel guilty 100 per cent of the time."

Cleo says explaining the financial situation in simple terms to her daughter helps.

"It's hard being a single parent money-wise and time-wise … but I always explain to my daughter that I must work so that we can do nice things, and she seems happy with that."

Allison also struggles to juggle work around childcare.

"I'm at home because I don't have any childcare at the moment, so I have to do my work from home. But when I do have childcare, I feel guilty using it! I once heard someone say why do people have children if they stick them in childcare all the time. It feels like a lose-lose situation where guilt is concerned!"

It would be nice to think that not many people share the view that you shouldn't have children if you put them in childcare; we assume that people who do think like that must have an endless pit of money and have never had to earn for their family. Lucky them, eh?

GUILT OVER MONEY

It can also be hard to not feel guilty when you see other families enjoying expensive day trips. As a one-income household there can be a lot less that we can do, all the standard day-to-day expenses may mean there is nothing left over to go on holidays or family experiences. It can also be gut-wrenching when the child gets to do fun things with their other parent, but not with you.

> **Ellie** explains:
> "It seems like I do the hard parenting work then 'Disneyland Dad' turns up with a new toy or takes her somewhere fun for the day and he's amazing in my child's eyes."

If you haven't heard of the phrase yet, a Disneyland Parent refers to a parent that gives the kid lots of presents, holidays and fun trips while the other parent is left to deal with the day-to-day parenting and more mundane things like discipline and homework. You've got to go easy on yourself, no matter what you're feeling guilty about you do not deserve to beat yourself up about it. You are doing the best you can in a difficult situation, and you are going to rock it.

GUILT FOR STRUGGLING WITH PARENTING

As a single mother you may be exhausted, overworked, never have enough time, stressed, and just really worn out. As a result, your parenting can be impacted. You may be tired, grumpy, not have time to sit down and play a game or watch TV together. You might choose more oven-ready meals or takeaways than you would like. You might miss getting through homework practice or reading with your child because you are: Just. So. Tired. All of this and more can lead to feelings of guilt: "I'm doing parenting wrong", "I'm not doing this well enough".

Katie noted how:

"*I often found myself rushing around in the evenings, doing a hundred tasks, or trying to reply to messages. I didn't feel I gave any quality time to my children and then would be so tired by bedtime that bedtime reading might get missed and I would go to bed feeling so, so guilty.*"

WHAT IS THE PURPOSE OF GUILT?

If we think about the function of guilt, in evolutionary terms why do we have guilt and how does guilt help us?

Well, guilt, by making us feel bad, highlights a problematic behaviour or situation that has happened, and thus makes us aware that we might be able to do something to repair a situation, resolve it, or make sure it doesn't happen again. If we act on this awareness, it can be helpful for us and others and help us not only resolve or repair problematic situations but also allow us to resolve the guilt. However, if we allow guilt to just be present and remain unchecked and unchallenged, all that happens is it festers and eats us up, making our mental health suffer. Guilt isn't designed to just sit with us forever, it is designed to be present, to help us, and to be let go.

> ### Misplaced Guilt
>
> Misplaced guilt can occur when we experience guilt in a way that is out of proportion to the situation, or we have an exaggerated sense of responsibility or blame for the situation leading to the guilt. Much of the guilt experienced during solo motherhood is misplaced guilt.

HOW TO MANAGE AND OVERCOME GUILT

Guilt, like shame, is a difficult emotion to process, release and let go of. However, there are tools and strategies that you can use to help you with this.

NOTICE

Learn to notice when guilt shows up for you; name the emotion, where you feel it in your body and how it makes you want to communicate and behave. When you notice this, you will be more able to make choices in how you want to respond to, contain and manage the guilt.

Notice and become familiar with your common guilt triggers, i.e. the situations that frequently make you feel guilty. Being aware of these will help you be prepared to use strategies to assuage those feelings when they show up.

UNDERSTAND

Take a moment to understand your guilt. What are you feeling guilty about? What thoughts are going through your mind about yourself, your children, your past, your future, your present? What is it about the situation you find yourself in that makes you feel guilty? Where does this guilt come from – is it from your views, or is it from other people's views (perceived or actual)? Write this down if you can. It is always effective to get your thoughts out on paper so you can tackle them more effectively.

QUESTION

Question or approach your thoughts in new ways, remembering the thinking biases from page 47. Ask yourself:

- "Are the thoughts and reasons behind my guilt really fair, valid and reasonable? Or am I jumping to conclusions, thinking in black and white, making assumptions about the situation?"
- "Am I actually to blame/responsible in this situation? Or am I being unnecessarily harsh, judgemental and self-critical?"
- "Is the amount of guilt I feel *really* appropriate in relation to the situation?"
- "I might feel responsible, but am I really? Did I *intentionally* cause this situation to come about?"
- "Who else is involved in this situation? What share of responsibility do they hold?"
- "Does it work for me to hold on to this guilt? Or does it keep me stuck, feeling terrible?"
- "Can I come up with a more reasonable, fair and valid thought about the situation?"
- "Can I forgive myself and be compassionate toward myself?"

ACTION

Following your self-questioning, what does this tell you about your actual level of blame or responsibility? If you feel you do need to make amends/apologize/take action in relation to the situation causing the guilt, take some time to think about what you can do.

If you are responsible, acknowledge this in as objective a way as possible and focus on what you can learn from the situation. What would you like to do differently in the future? How can you avoid making this mistake or taking this course of action again in the future? Learning from our mistakes is far more effective a strategy than just making ourselves feel guilty without action.

Can you separate out the behaviour (what happened) from the emotion (the guilt)? The behaviour or situation has happened, and can't be changed; the guilt serves no purpose now except to make you feel bad. You can learn from it and/or you can allow yourself to be forgiven, and/or you can acknowledge this guilt is misplaced, or out of proportion, or unnecessarily harsh and ultimately unhelpful.

To forgive yourself, you need to be self-compassionate and kind to yourself about any mistakes you may have made, intentionally or otherwise. Remind yourself that allowing guilt to be present without challenge or meaningful action serves no purpose. You do not deserve to be surrounded by guilt forever. It is okay to be able to forgive yourself.

LETTING GUILT GO

Once you have noticed, understood and taken action over your guilt, let yourself reach the conclusion that "Actually it is time – it is okay for me to let this guilt go". Giving yourself permission is an essential part of the process. It will be hard to let guilt go if you are actually secretly thinking I deserve this, I should feel guilty, I need to feel guilty. So check in with yourself – are there any barriers to letting this guilt go? Is there anything stopping you? If so, go back through the steps above.

Letting go: The aim is that every time you notice the guilt showing up you say to yourself something like, "Here is guilt showing up. I know it is time to let this go now, it isn't helping me, and it is only serving to keep me miserable and stuck. It's time to let it go and stop beating myself up." Then imagine physically letting that guilt go – you might want to give yourself a little shake as you gently shake it off so it is free from you, you might want to imagine it drifting away into the sky like a waft of cloud. It's okay if it doesn't disappear completely – it might hang around, and that's normal. You just don't have to be burdened by it. Just acknowledge it is there and refocus on you, your children, your life, and the next meaningful thing you want to do.

Over time, new guilt might show up and you might need to go through these steps with the new guilt. That's okay. Just work through it. If, despite all the above, your guilt is overwhelming, intense and problematic, then please do reach out for help and support with a counsellor, clinical or counselling psychologist or couples/family therapist.

HOW TO SIT WITH YOUR CHILDREN'S PAIN AND LOSS WITHOUT TAKING ON THE EMOTIONAL GUILT

When your child says or does something that triggers your feelings of guilt, take a deep breath and try the following strategies.

NOTICE
Notice and acknowledge the guilt that has just shown up for you.

UNDERSTAND
Remind yourself gently and kindly that it is okay for your children to feel different and difficult emotions. Being part of a single-parent family can be a difficult experience for them. And the reality is, even if this difficult experience wasn't in their life, there would be other difficult things presenting themselves. We cannot control the challenges our children may face, but we can help them to grow through those challenges and support

them to be emotionally flexible, resilient, responsive and self-compassionate – to help them understand how they are thinking and feeling and to teach them skills to manage this.

Remind yourself gently and kindly that you cannot make the situation better for your child, in the sense that there is no magic wand to return to a two-parent household, and they will feel difficult emotions during difficult times. But you can help them through this, support them with their emotions, without "fixing" things or taking on the guilt of their emotions yourself.

FOCUS ON YOUR CHILD

Take another deep breath and imagine with the breath that you are making space between you and the guilt so you can focus on what your child has just said or done and be there to listen and acknowledge their feeling. Imagine guilt is like a little goblin; it can sit there while you talk to your child but you don't have to be completely hooked/consumed by it right now. Focus on this conversation with your child, and help them to notice and name how they are feeling, and let them talk if they want to. Try using similar statements to those below.

- "I can hear you are feeling sad about this ...."
- "It sounds like you are missing Mummy/Daddy today."
- "I understand this must feel really hard."
- "Thank you for sharing that, how are you feeling right now?"

Remember to offer physical comfort too if they want this – hug, hold hands, stroke their hair.

If appropriate, acknowledge how the situation makes you feel too – acknowledge when you also find a situation hard or sad; for example, you might say something like, "I can hear this makes you feel sad. It makes me feel sad too sometimes." But don't share your feelings of guilt with them, as this is not for your child to bear, and is something for you to work through in your own adult space.

Let them know it is normal and understandable to feel what they feel or have the questions they do. Let them know it is okay to talk to you or to ask questions – you might not always have all the answers but you will do your best. Try not to make topics off limits. At the same time, if you are finding the conversation overwhelming, try strategies such as deep breathing, grounding and reminding yourself you will be okay, that this is hard but you can do this. If the conversation still feels overwhelming, share this with them in a gentle age-appropriate way; for example, "Oh, Mummy is feeling a bit sad too right now, shall we just have a cuddle for a moment, or shall we put on a song we both like and just have some quiet time for a minute and then chat some more?" Keep in mind your child might not want to talk through things at this very moment, and let them know that is okay, but you are there if and when they would like to.

Once you have listened, validated, supported, comforted, see if you can offer any practical support; for example, "When I feel like this there are certain things that help me, can I show you?" or "Do you want us to think about anything you might like to do to help with this?" It might be they want to look at photos and talk about them, or phone the other parent; it might be to do some art, or writing, or playing a silly game.

Once you have gone through all this and your child is settled and occupied, if you need, take some time to go through the strategies above to help yourself.

SELF-COMPASSIONATE STATEMENTS AS AN ANTIDOTE TO GUILT

- "I am a single mum and my child and I are going to have to navigate some new situations. Some may be good; some may be difficult. But we can do this and hold our heads up high while we do so."
- "I (or we, if including ex-partner) did not intend to be in this situation. We find ourselves here now and the best we can do is focus on making this as good for all of us as we can."
- "I had to make some tough decisions for the sake of me, my mental health and my family. However hard it is, I can remember I was trying to do the right thing."
- "Family comes in all shapes and sizes. There is not one way to be a family anymore. As a single parent and as a co-parent I can still offer my child a loving home and help him/her feel safe and secure and loved."
- "Life does not always go to plan. This isn't what I wished and hoped for, but it is my life and I will make the best of it. It may be tricky sometimes, but I can teach myself and my child strength and resilience."

Understanding Your Experience of Guilt

To better understand your relationship with guilt, practise the following reflective exercise as often as necessary, and keep these notes safe to remind yourself of them when things become difficult.

1. Identify an area or situation that you know triggers your guilt.
2. To help you build a clearer understanding of the guilt and how you can respond to it, work your way through the strategies detailed in page 102 of:
   - Notice
   - Understand
   - Question
   - Action
   - Let go
3. Take some time to notice how this exercise makes you feel.
4. How does it feel to consider allowing yourself to let go of guilt?
5. How could things be different if you felt less guilty? What could you do differently, and how could this positively impact on you?

5

ANXIETY, PANIC AND OVERWHELM

For anyone prone to anxiety, it can worsen when facing single parenthood. Or you might experience it for the first time, and this can be terrifying. This chapter gives an insight into what living with anxiety as a single mother is like, from an increase in worry, to anxiety-induced insomnia because of a fear of falling asleep and never waking up, to full-blown panic attacks when your child stays at their other parent's house.

Anxiety is a normal human reaction to something worrying or unnerving; however, when it is happening regularly and impacting on your life it can become problematic, and you will need to find ways to manage this yourself or with help and support.

WHAT IS ANXIETY?

Anxiety is a natural emotion that all of us will experience. It can be useful, healthy and, at times, entirely appropriate. It is a primitive response designed for self-protection. When we feel anxious, our awareness of a potential risk or threat increases, and makes us consider what we need to do to protect ourselves or others to stay safe. For example, if your child develops a high temperature, your anxiety/worry will show up and help you take action to check his temperature, give him medicine, seek medical advice and so on, which helps protect you all.

As individuals, we will all experience situations that trigger our anxiety, and we will all have times when we experience anxiety as a parent and, of course, as a single parent. As we are all different, what may trigger anxiety for one person, may not trigger anxiety for someone else. This is important to note because it helps us understand that sometimes it is not the *situation* that determines whether we feel anxious or not, but *our own personal reaction* to the situation. For example, in the playground two children are hanging off the high bars; one parent is frantically hovering underneath trying to get them down, calling out advice and instructions to help get their child to the ground safely; the other parent sits back watching their child, occasionally advising them to "hold on" or "don't climb there", but otherwise letting their child navigate the situation themselves. The situation is the same, but these two parents are responding very differently as their anxiety levels are being triggered differently.

In short, manageable bursts of anxiety are okay. However, there are times when anxiety can show up excessively and alert us to threat unnecessarily or unhelpfully and repeatedly. Anxiety can begin to make us overestimate the threat or likelihood of danger. It can begin to be present in your life for hours, days, weeks, perhaps rising and falling, but creeping into your thoughts and feelings more times than it doesn't. This is when it can start to become problematic and may begin to tip over into a being a mental health issue with which you may benefit from help and support.

Anxiety as a mental health condition can, if needed, be diagnosed by your personal doctor, a psychiatrist or suitably trained mental health professional. Generalized Anxiety Disorder (GAD) is one of the most common types of diagnoses given.

GAD is when a person experiences worry and anxiety in everyday life and finds it difficult to stop worrying and feeling anxious about a range of different issues or situations. This anxiety affects their work, parenting and social life.

There are a range of other conditions or diagnoses that fit under an umbrella of anxiety diagnoses, such as health anxiety, obsessive compulsive disorder (OCD), panic disorder and phobias. If you have previously experienced any of these anxiety conditions, and then go through a stressful experience, such as a relationship breakdown, divorce, separation, becoming a single parent, and all the challenges that experience brings, then it is easy for previously experienced anxiety conditions to be triggered or exacerbated through the stress.

AN ALTERNATIVE TO DIAGNOSIS

Rather than viewing anxiety as a disorder, it can be helpful to consider anxiety as existing on a continuum from not anxious to severely anxious. People may fluctuate along this continuum over the course of their life. Within this framework, anxiety is understood as an understandable response to stress and trauma in a person's life, which at times may become difficult or overwhelming, at which point support may be sought to help them make sense of and manage this.

So anxiety in your journey as a single mum may show up briefly (for example, when you have to walk into a social event for the first time on your own), or for short periods of time (for example, during the separation, or the move to a new home), or (and particularly if you may have experienced anxiety in your life prior to this) it may show up more regularly and consistently for days and weeks, and become problematic in your ability to function day to day.

THINGS YOU SHOULD KNOW ABOUT ANXIETY

1. You are not crazy.
2. Anxiety is a sign that your body and mind is feeling overwhelmed and under threat (whether real or imagined).
3. Ignoring anxiety or trying to suppress it won't make it go away.
4. Anxiety is treatable and you will get through this.
5. Anxiety as a mental health condition is very common. Between 10 and 20 per cent of people experience an anxiety condition.
6. Changing the way you think and act can help reduce anxiety.
7. There are therapies which can help reduce anxiety and teach you more effective ways to manage it.
8. For some people medication is really helpful for treating anxiety.

HOW WE EXPERIENCE ANXIETY

We experience anxiety when our body and mind are triggered by an event and feel under threat – we believe we may be in danger or have a worry about something bad happening. Anxiety affects how we *feel (emotions)*, how we *think (thoughts)*, how our body *feels (physical symptoms)*, and how we *behave*.

WHAT TRIGGERS ANXIETY?

As with anger, anxiety can be triggered by external or internal events. External events may be your child not coming home from school when you were expecting them, or being in a social situation as a single parent for the first time. Internal events may include thinking about being a single parent, thinking about having to do something as a single parent, or thinking about your child having to meet your ex's new girlfriend. Internal triggers can be thoughts, memories, images of past or future. In this way, anxiety can be triggered when we wake up in the morning or when we are sitting having a cup of tea – any time our thoughts start hooking into anxieties and worries in our mind.

HOW WE FEEL WHEN WE ARE ANXIOUS

We can have a range of emotions that we connect with anxiety – we can feel anxious, nervous, worried, panicked – but may also have additional emotions such as fearful, irritated, angry, scared, terrified, stressed, an impending sense of doom or of something bad happening.

HOW WE THINK WHEN ANXIOUS

We can experience anxious and worrying thoughts when we think about the current situation, the past, the future, or about ourselves or others. These anxious thoughts can hook us in and end up going round and round our head, spiralling into more and more anxious thoughts. You can go from zero to a hundred really quickly, starting from a small worrying thought and quickly jumping to another, catastrophizing and imagining terrible worst-case scenarios. Those unhelpful thinking habits or common thinking biases that we talked about in the chapter on anger, definitely show up here.

BIASED THINKING – ANXIETY

- Catastrophizing – thinking or predicting the worst about any situation; for example, "I can't get hold of my child, something awful must have happened."

- Making mountains out of molehills – taking a small issue and imagining a far greater issue.
- Jumping to conclusions without evidence; for example, "Everyone must think I am a failure for being a single mum."
- Making assumptions – assuming what other people are thinking and assuming this must be the worst thing, or a critical judgement on you or those close to you.
- Creating "what ifs" – getting caught up in endless alternative scenarios about the current situation or future, or even – futilely – going over past events.
- Engaging in emotional reasoning – feeling anxious, so therefore there must be something to be anxious about;
- Overgeneralizing; for example, thinking, if your first social event as a single mum wasn't a roaring success, that "I'm never going to be able to enjoy socializing again."

Intrusive Thoughts

When thoughts become persistent, repetitive and distressing – coming into your mind when you don't want them – they can be described as intrusive thoughts. Attempts to push them away or get rid of them often make them come back stronger. Intrusive thoughts are extremely common. Studies have found that over 90 per cent of the general population experience intrusive thoughts at some time or another. However, for some people they can be debilitating, so developing the right strategies to tackle these is crucial. The most important way we can change our relationship with intrusive thoughts is by knowing that just because we have had the thought, it doesn't mean it is true or will come true, and also by knowing that having the thought doesn't mean anything about you, or about what is going to happen. It is just a thought. An unpleasant one, but still, just a thought.

HOW WE FEEL PHYSICALLY WHEN ANXIOUS

When we experience anxiety our nervous system activates our sympathetic nervous system and our body goes into fight or flight mode. This is a physiological process that causes us to feel symptoms such as a racing heart, quickened breathing, constricted throat, churning stomach or butterflies in the tummy or nausea, shaking/trembling, dizziness, feeling faint, weakness, tiredness but also insomnia, sweating, noise sensitivity. These symptoms can make you feel very agitated, restless or tense, and it can be difficult to eat.

HOW WE BEHAVE WHEN ANXIOUS

The most common ways anxiety affects our behaviour is through avoidance (of the anxious situation) or withdrawal (withdrawing away from people or situations). Rumination is also another common behavioural process; this is where we go over and over and over the same thoughts or issues. Other anxious behaviours include reassurance-seeking or checking behaviours.

PANIC ATTACKS

Panic attacks are one aspect of anxiety. Not everyone who experiences anxiety will experience panic attacks, and you can be very anxious without ever having a panic attack. However, for some people they are a common part of the anxiety experience.

A panic attack is a fear response, an intense anxiety reaction. The body will suddenly experience an intense fear/ panic reaction which can feel like it comes out of the blue and happens fast. All the physical symptoms of anxiety described above can be present in a panic attack, but appear much more quickly and intensely. For example, where breathing and heart rate can quicken in anxiety, this can *rapidly* speed up in a panic attack.

During a panic attack a person might think that they can't breathe, are going to faint, lose control, or that they will have a heart attack and die. This is because the physiological reaction in the body, the rapid fight or flight response and sharp increase in adrenalin, causes the physical symptoms that make you feel and think that something terrible must be happening to you.

Importantly, none of these terrifying thoughts are true, but when a person believes these scary thoughts, this feeds back into the anxiety and fear cycle and stops the symptoms from receding and in fact escalates the symptoms, keeping them going.

Experiencing regular panic attacks can lead to withdrawal and avoidance to try to prevent them from occurring. Seeking therapy for how to manage a panic attack can be really helpful.

How to Deal with a Panic Attack

1. Practise deep breathing regularly so you will feel more able to use this strategy when a panic attack begins.
2. Focus on breathing a little slower with each breath.
3. Ground yourself – push your feet into the floor, name what is happening: "I am feeling panic. I can feel this in my body. This is really unpleasant, but I can cope with this."
4. Look around you and focus on something you can see, hear or touch or smell.

5. Remind yourself that this experience is unpleasant but cannot harm you – this is just your body reacting because it *thinks* you are in danger, so is sending lots of adrenalin round your system.
6. Remind yourself that it will pass. It may be unpleasant, but it will pass.
7. As you do the above, notice as your body and mind slowly calm down.

As much as we'd like to offer you a priceless piece of advice that will stop anxiety and panic in its tracks, sometimes all we can do is ride it out. Let the panic attack happen, acknowledge the thoughts and feelings it brings, breathe, and reflect on it afterwards. This gets a lot easier the more panic attacks you suffer from, as you can remind yourself how you've gotten through these feelings time and time again, and you will get through this one too.

A NOTE ABOUT STRESS, BURNOUT AND BEING OVERWHELMED

Anxiety can show up for all of us when we feel under stress and overwhelmed. We can experience stress when we are in a number of situations that are difficult or challenging or put pressure on us, and these start to affect how we are thinking or feeling.

As a single mother of course there are lots of areas of potential stress in our lives – being a single parent, coping as a single parent, dealing with your ex-partner, dealing with your ex's new relationships, dealing with the impact the separation has on your child, and so on.

Stress by itself isn't a diagnosis, and there may be some differing ideas of what stress exactly is. Stress can cause anxiety, it can cause low mood. It can certainly cause you to feel overwhelmed and if it is ongoing, completely burnt out.

Stress can make you worried, anxious, irritated, snappy, angry, panicked. It can make you struggle to function as effectively as you normally would and makes everything feel harder to manage. It can make it harder to switch off. It can lead to headaches, chest pain, tummy problems, fatigue and more. Stress can lead you to unhealthy habits – drinking more, smoking more, eating more or not at all, working too hard or not sleeping. Stress can lead to burnout, where you just can't cope anymore. You may find yourself bursting into tears easily, finding simple tasks challenging, being exhausted, feeling overwhelmed all the time.

If you are feeling any of these things, it is important to get support and to distinguish between stress, burnout and mental health conditions such as anxiety or depression.

However, we can all help ourselves by being honest with ourselves and keeping an eye on the amount of stressful situations we are facing. If we do this, we can also take time to find ways to reduce our stressors or to increase our self-care to make it possible to deal with these stressors.

STORIES OF ANXIETY IN SINGLE MOTHERHOOD

Everyone experiences anxiety in different ways. We have shared some stories from some of our amazing single mothers of their experiences of anxiety. From anxiety showing up when you first separate, to when you have to attend social occasions on your own or when you leave your child for the first time.

*When **Bella's** husband left her anxiety went through the roof.*

"I thought everyone was judging me, I felt horribly ashamed that I had done something wrong. I felt like everyone was talking about me, and even when I went to different places I felt like I had a sign above my head saying I am a single mum. The first time we went out for a meal just me and the children I felt so anxious about what the waitress and other people were thinking. One of the waitresses made a comment about how their dad would be proud of their good behaviour and I didn't know what to say. It felt terrible."

Katie *had her first experience of bad anxiety after her separation.*

"I've never really been someone who gets anxious. But after the separation, when we were living in the new home and I was spending days and weeks trying to get everything done – parenting, working, coping – I would find myself feeling increasingly stressed, overwhelmed, anxious. I would wake up in the night with intense anxiety – I would be convinced I'd forgotten to lock the doors, or hadn't put the children to bed, or that something terrible was about to happen. I remember one Sunday sitting in my kitchen thinking about my situation and everything that was going on – my ex-partner had annoyed me, my children were being challenging, I had too much to do – and I could feel the anxiety just creeping up, building up in my chest, and I just had to sit and stop. It was too much."

When my anxiety was really bad, and my son was at his dad's house I would spend the whole time thinking about bad things that could happen. I would message morning and night, or whenever I felt worried; but I would also get myself so worked up if he didn't respond. I went on a dreamy holiday without my son; it was hot and lovely and I spent the day at the beach. However, when I got back to my hotel room I started freaking out because I hadn't heard from my son or his dad. I texted and called, but had no replies, so I convinced myself that something bad had happened. I was spiralling and contemplating all kinds of things, like how far away I was from the airport and how soon I could get a flight home. I ended up calling my ex's girlfriend who assured me everything was okay. When I came out of the panic state, I was absolutely exhausted and all I could do was sleep for a few hours. Part of my anxiety involves me feeling completely fatigued. Once a panic attack is over, I physically can't do anything for a while as my brain is just so drained and my body will not play ball. **Amy**

Frankie *suffers with anxiety when her daughter stays at her dad's house.*

"When my daughter started going to her dad's house at night the anxiety was totally amplified because he didn't want to communicate with me when she was there. He would think that it's because I don't trust him, but it had nothing to do with his parental responsibility, it was about my anxiety and how it presents itself."

While constant checking up on our children must be pretty annoying for our ex-partners, at the time all we want is continual reassurance that our children are safe. However, it's important to recognize that reassurance seeking is part of unhelpful anxiety behaviours and this can have a negative effect on the co-parenting relationship, and it may be worth seeking help for anxiety early on to avoid this.

>   **Bella** suffers with catastrophic thoughts.
>   "When something particularly stressful or triggering has happened, I'll visualize catastrophic things. It's not a fleeting thought, more of a play-by-play of what could happen. It's like a runaway train once it's started, I can't stop it."

When these thoughts come into your head, try to remember that they are anxious thoughts automatically generated in your brain, and not anything that you are choosing.

> When my anxiety is really out of control, I'll imagine the worst possible things that could happen and spiral from there. I'll feel completely on edge, my hands go clammy, and I feel sick. I used to hyperventilate, but after years of anxiety I have managed to get that side of things under control with the help of yogic breathing. **Amy**

When you're suffering from anxiety, it can be difficult to hide this from your child. When Amy is anxious she can grind her teeth without realizing it until her son asks what she's chewing! When anxious, you might be easily irritated with your child over little things, such as having to ask them repeatedly to put their shoes away. Being the one person that has to do the day-in, day-out routine with the children is completely draining, so it's no wonder we snap or lose patience when anxiety is playing up.

> **Allison** has also been struggling with the anxious mum life.
> "Sometimes when I'm anxious I'll be snappy just because I'm using up all of my energy to look after the kids and they're not reciprocating or appreciating anything … because they're kids."

> **Cleo** really struggled with her daughter's behaviour when she and her ex broke up.
> "If she was being naughty, I'd end up having a breakdown because I just felt so anxious, like I couldn't deal with it all on my own. I felt so very alone, especially as I have no family around."

While we've all had our moments when the kids have been naughty, your response can emphasize your need for support during this time. If you don't seek support or help with your anxiety, it is likely to spiral and become harder to deal with.

HOW TO OVERCOME YOUR ANXIETY

KNOW YOUR TRIGGERS

The first thing you need to work out is what your anxiety triggers are, as once you've worked out what these are, you can start finding ways to be prepared for and manage these situations. Keeping a diary can help you identify triggers (see next point).

EXTERNAL TRIGGERS

External triggers in solo motherhood may include:

- Being in a school or social situation as a single parent surrounded by two-parent families
- Being overwhelmed with too many parenting/work/life tasks to complete
- Realizing you have forgotten something important for your child (for example, costume for school, missed an appointment)
- Navigating potentially dangerous activities alone; for example, riding a scooter or bike, or swimming in the sea
- When your child is sick in the night and you know you have to work the next day
- When your child goes to stay at their other parent's home for the first time or for a longer period of time than usual
- When you go out and leave the children with a sitter
- When you are late to pick them up from school or nursery as life/work tasks delayed you
- When you tell your child about the separation/new homes

INTERNAL TRIGGERS

Internal triggers in solo motherhood may include:

- Thinking about how you will cope in the future
- Thinking about if your children will be okay with the separation/new homes/new girlfriend
- Thinking about if you are going to be a good-enough parent
- Thinking about all the tasks you have to do, or about an upcoming event
- Remembering horrible experiences from the past
- Thinking about being alone
- Thinking about what other people might be thinking of you

- Noticing heart racing or feeling sick, or feeling unwell and beginning to worry about your health or mental health
- Worrying about getting poorly or something bad happening while you're on your own with your child

UNDERSTAND IT

You may want to see a therapist to help you understand your anxiety, or you might feel able to do this yourself by following the steps below and through guided reading.

Keep a Diary

1. Over the course of a week, make a note of when you feel anxious. Keep track of what is happening when you begin feeling anxious – the situation you are in, who you are with and what the external and/or internal trigger could be.
2. Try to write down the thoughts you have when you feel anxious – what you think about yourself, your life, your past, your future; as well as what you think others are thinking of you.
3. Notice and note how your body feels when you feel anxious – do you feel it in your tummy, your chest, your throat?
4. Notice how you behave or want to behave when you feel anxious.
5. After a week, see if you can notice any themes or patterns in the anxiety triggers and in how anxiety makes you think, feel and behave. Doing this can help you better understand and predict your own anxiety experience.

SOOTHE THE PHYSICAL SYMPTOMS

"Take a deep breath. Just breathe." You've probably had people say this to you when you have been feeling anxious, and for some it can feel like the equivalent of saying "Calm down" – which never calms anyone down!

However, understanding the science behind this can be helpful. When we are anxious, deep, calm breathing can be really useful and effective. The reason for this is that when we take slow, deep breaths we activate our parasympathetic nervous system, which is where we calm, soothe, rest and digest. When we are anxious or panicky our sympathetic nervous system (our fight or flight system) is activated, and so deep breathing helps us move back into a calming balance by activating the parasympathetic nervous system instead, and can reduce the anxious physical symptoms we may be experiencing.

THE PRINCIPLES OF DEEP BREATHING

- Take a slow, deep breath in through your nose, keeping your chest as still as you can and breathing from the bottom of your lungs, allowing your tummy and sides to expand as the air fills your lungs.
- Hold for a moment if it feels comfortable.
- Breathe out slowly through your nose or mouth. If you can, make this out breath a little longer than the in breath.

Tip: If you are feeling anxious and panicky, you might find it helps to breathe out first, pushing the air out of your lungs, making space, before you try to breathe in deeply.

You can also try adding in any one of the following:

- Imagine a cool, calming colour washing through you as you breathe in.

- Use a scent stick with a calming smell as you breathe.
- Open your arms out to the side as you breathe in and bring them together into a prayer position as you breathe out.
- As you take your deep breaths, visualize your body calming, your heart rate slowing.
- Choose a mantra to say to yourself as you breathe (for example, "Calm", "Relax", "I can do this", "I'm okay", "This is hard, but I can get through this").

You can use this technique when you are feeling anxious, but you can also practise this regularly during the day (for example, when you wake up, when you are boiling the kettle, when you are sitting in the car waiting for school pick-up) to keep your nervous system feeling calmer/soothed and to be more able to use this when you feel stressed.

CALM THE MIND, MANAGE WORRIES AND UNHOOK FROM ANXIOUS THOUGHTS

Anxious thoughts can swirl round your mind, making it feel very difficult to be calm, breathe, sleep and take part in activities. Tackling our thoughts can be crucial to any of the other strategies working well.

There are lots of ways to tackle anxious thoughts, and if you want to learn more about this, do consider the guided reading options for anxiety or seek therapy support options. Some ideas you can try to include:

- Learn mindfulness skills to begin to notice your thoughts when they happen. Take a moment to imagine you are looking in and watching your thoughts as they roll through your mind. What do you see? Try to notice them by saying: "I notice I am having the thought that …".

- Once you have noticed your thoughts, check in with those thinking errors/biased thinking, to see if any of those are present.
- Remember, anxious thoughts usually overestimate the danger and threat of how likely it is a bad thing will happen.
- Remind yourself that anxious thoughts aren't necessarily true, factual or accurate. See if you can challenge your thoughts. What is the evidence that this thought is true? What is a more balanced, more likely, more reasonable way of thinking about the situation? If you knew this thought wasn't true, what would you say to a friend or your child who was thinking this?
- Remind yourself that just because you feel anxious doesn't mean that there is actually any danger/risk or bad thing happening. We can feel anxious purely because of the worries in our mind. Anxiety can come from our thoughts, so if we think differently, we will feel differently.
- Problem-solve your worries. Find a time of day to write down everything that is worrying you. Go through each worry and ask yourself if there is anything you can do about this worry. If yes, ask yourself, *should you* actually do anything about this worry (is it your place to do anything, will it actually improve the situation, are you just reassurance seeking)? If yes again, plan what you can do and take action. If no, focus on ways you can let your thoughts go as dwelling on them won't help you.
- Ask yourself: "Will it help me to listen to this thought, to be controlled by it, to believe it? Or will it make me more anxious and make me act in anxious ways?"
- Try and hold on to the fair and balanced thoughts, and focus on calming yourself down – both body and mind. Remind yourself that the negative thought is due to your anxiety

being on high alert, and calming your anxiety is the focus, not the thing your mind has latched on to worry about.

MAKE SPACE AND LET IT BE

Often when we feel anxious we want to get rid of the feelings it arouses. However, therapy approaches have found that when we turn *toward* the anxiety – notice it, make space for it, allow it to be there, accept that it may turn up in your life, breathe into it and around it, sit with it – then we can actually teach ourselves to be able to cope with it, contain it and refocus on what is important to us, despite the anxiety still being there.

> **Allison** suffers from panic attacks, so when she feels these coming on, she will give herself some time to sit with them. "I felt really anxious the other day, so I gave myself 20 minutes, let the anxiety happen and just acknowledged what was triggering me. I worked out that it was because I felt like I had so much to do with so little time. So, I made a list of things I can do now and then things that I can do later. Then I called a friend and went for a walk."

Giving herself that time to make space for the anxiety and work out what was causing the anxiety helped Allison to stop spiralling and put in effective measures to overcome the feelings. Fresh air and companionship can also often do wonders for anxiety.

HELP YOURSELF SLEEP BETTER

Sleep often becomes problematic when we are anxious. We might have bad dreams, night terrors, wake with anxiety or find it hard to sleep. Anxious thoughts often whirl around our heads at night. Some ways of tackling this include:

- Remind yourself gently but assertively that worrying about things at night will only make you feel worse and will not help you sleep. Keep a notepad by your bed to make a note of anything you are thinking about that you want to address in the morning.

- As soon as you notice anxious thoughts creeping into your mind, remind yourself of the point above and gently guide your mind to a more neutral topic. This might be imagining a calming place you would love to be, or doing something mundane like naming the players in your local football team.
- Use a breathing exercise or try a sleep meditation app (Calm, Headspace); or try a progressive relaxation exercise (where you tense then relax each part of your body) to help you to become calm and soothed ready for sleep.
- If you can't sleep after 25 minutes or so, it is best to get up and sit somewhere in a quiet place, with dim lights and do something quiet and non-stimulating (read a book, listen to music) until you are ready to try and get to sleep again (there are some good sleep science theories to back this up).
- If you wake with physical anxiety, focus on calming your mind and body using the breathing exercise on page 126 and by talking to yourself in a calming way.
- If you are still struggling with your sleep, there is a great, free, online sleep self-help programme at www.sleepio.com.
- If you are experiencing nightmares, there is a helpful technique called the Dream Completion technique which you can try (see Useful Resources).

CHANGE YOUR BEHAVIOURS, FIND NEW WAYS OF RESPONDING
Reduce Avoidance and Social Withdrawal

Aim to notice when anxiety tries to make you withdraw and avoid, and ultimately aim to do the opposite. The principle is that when we avoid/withdraw, we keep the anxiety going by teaching ourselves that we can't cope and the only option is to get out. Then the next time the anxiety or similar situation arises, we just want to get out again, and the pattern just keeps repeating. We never learn to cope with the situation and thus realize that anxiety could reduce by staying in the situation. Often when we go into a feared situation, the anxiety goes up at first, and then slowly comes down. And over time, if we keep putting ourselves in the feared situation, the fear may reduce completely.

Reduce Reassurance-Seeking or Checking Behaviours

When we seek reassurance for our anxiety or carry out checking behaviours (for example, repetitively texting to check on children), we get a temporary relief from the anxiety, but over time this slowly fades and the anxiety builds again, and we have to check/seek reassurance all over again. As with the avoidance situation, by seeking reassurance or checking, we are inadvertently keeping the anxiety going. The way to reduce the anxiety is to stop checking or seeking reassurance and focus on helping ourselves cope with the anxious thoughts and feelings by calming and soothing ourselves using the strategies above.

Reduce Rumination

Try to write your worries down rather than letting them ruminate through your mind over and over. Once you have written them down you can use the thought strategies outlined above to help you tackle the thoughts. Then practise letting the thoughts go.

Letting Thoughts Go

There are lots of ways to practise letting thoughts go rather than staying hooked and caught up in them. Letting go using mindfulness doesn't mean the thoughts will necessarily disappear, but it does mean you learn to stop listening to them or focusing on them.

You can imagine you are listening to a radio tuned to Anxiety FM and just imagine the thoughts rumbling around in the background as you carry on with your day. You can also imagine letting them go using imagery. Imagine the thoughts are leaves dropping into a stream and floating away. Or as they pop into your mind, imagine each thought written on a balloon, and letting the balloons float away. You might just notice them pop into your mind and gently waft them past. They might keep popping in but you can keep letting them go.

LOOK AFTER YOURSELF

To help reduce overall anxiety it can help to look at the bigger picture: practise self-care, take a break, accept help from others, take time just for you, get outside, reduce overall stressors where possible. These can all help reduce your overall stress levels and, in response, your anxiety levels too.

Tell someone how you're feeling; it can be hard for us to analyse our triggers and thoughts but talking to a friend or someone you trust can help you see how realistic (or not) your worries are.

Limit your alcohol and caffeine intake, as both are known to increase anxiety levels.

REFOCUS

Sometimes what you need to do is refocus yourself. Whether it's having a warm bath, petting an animal or going for a walk, opting for this technique can help to stop you from spiralling. You may have to try different things to work out what is effective for you.

Kasia explains:

"Sometimes what will work is a nice hot bath with candles and oils, other times it will be screaming into a pillow or calling a friend. There's not one thing that will always work, every time. It reminds me of colicky babies, sometimes what *works is driving over the same speed bump with a pram over and over again, but the next day that won't work."*

In short, anxiety is not a one-size-fits-all situation. What works for one, might make another feel worse; but it's important to explore ways to personally deal with these emotions when they arise.

"IN THE MOMENT" TIPS FOR COPING WITH ANXIETY

- Change your environment – go outside for a walk, do something completely different to what you were doing when you started feeling anxious.
- Splash your face and hands with cold water.
- Try mindful breathing: 4 x 4 breathing is a popular technique: Count to four as you breathe in and to four as you breathe out.
- Name how you are feeling and practise kind self-talk – I am anxious right now and I can get through this.
- Have a warm, soothing bath or a cold shower.
- Do an intense burst of exercise (ten star jumps for example) or take part in exercise you love (like going for a run).
- Breathe into and make space for the anxiety and remind yourself you can carry on whether anxiety shows up or not.

THERAPY

There are a range of therapeutic options for anxiety. Therapy can help you understand and contain your anxiety, and can help by giving you active strategies to help you respond to your anxiety in new ways and thus reducing it to a manageable level.

Having to live your life around anxiety is not fun. It can feel like the anxiety is in control of whether you're having a good day or a bad day and can make your life feel pretty small. Changing your mindset can do wonders in the long run. An hour each week of just being able to tell a friendly face absolutely everything and anything you have been thinking or feeling can be bliss. And beyond just listening, your therapist will be able to give you some honest advice and useful ways of dealing with your anxiety. Hopefully, you will be able to work out when your anxiety started, what events throughout your past heightened it and find ways of thinking about your anxiety in a different way.

Frankie found therapy a life saver.

"Using my savings to pay for therapy was the best decision I ever made. One of the techniques I've learnt from therapy is to think about each worry and work out whether it is a past worry, a present worry or a future worry, and how likely it is to happen. If it's a present worry, then I put in place things to help me stop worrying. If it's a future worry, I visualize a timeline of where it is in the future and try to think of it as a worry I will get to when I need to so that I don't feel completely overwhelmed."

Therapy can get quite expensive if you see a therapist privately. However, do look into whether you can access any free government-funded therapy services. Some charities can also help with therapy.

There are multiple therapy approaches, and we will talk you through some of these here:

Counselling

Counselling sessions with a trained counsellor will give you the space to talk and be listened to. Sometimes this is enough to help you express and contain your anxiety.

However, you may want to try a more active therapy approach to help you learn a range of new skills and understanding of anxiety. In this case you may try any of the following:

Cognitive Behavioural Therapy (CBT)

CBT can be provided by a trained CBT therapist, or a clinical or counselling psychologist. CBT is an approach that helps you understand how anxiety makes you think, feel and behave, and gives you strategies, skills and knowledge to help you manage your thoughts, physical symptoms and behaviours.

Acceptance and Commitment Therapy (ACT)

ACT can be provided by a trained ACT therapist, often a clinical or counselling psychologist. ACT is a therapy that helps us acknowledge when anxiety shows up and how it makes us feel and behave. It helps us understand anxiety is a normal human emotion and how to make space for it in your life; it teaches skills to help you ground yourself when anxiety shows up and step back (defuse) from the anxious thoughts, and to make meaningful choices for how you want to behave and the person you want to be, whether anxiety shows up or not.

Eye Movement Desensitization and Reprocessing (EMDR)

EMDR can be provided by a trained EMDR practitioner. This approach was originally developed for PTSD, but has been found to be helpful for a range of mental health difficulties. Find out more about EMDR at www.emdrassociation.org.uk.

Applied Relaxation

A trained therapist can help you with learning applied relaxation techniques, or you can learn these yourself. Applied relaxation helps you to recognize the symptoms of anxiety in the body and how to relax the body when it becomes tense with anxiety. You learn to practise relaxing the body and the different muscles, and then you put this into practice when anxiety rises up. Passive (focusing on each part of the body and imagining it relaxing) and progressive (tensing and relaxing each part of the body in turn) relaxation exercises help you learn to relax the body. Guided imagery relaxation exercises, such as listening to someone talk you through a walk in the woods or along the beach, can help you relax the mind and body. You can find lots of these exercises on YouTube.

Self-help

You could also explore your own guided self-help or psycho-education to help you understand anxiety and how to respond to it. Find some suggestions in the Useful Resources.

MEDICATION

You might feel like you've tried everything you can and still not feel any better, which is when medication may be worth considering. While there can still be some stigma around taking medication, it is a lot more common for people to use anxiety medication nowadays.

Individually, some people find medication helps, whilst others find it unhelpful. This is an individual experience and you need to explore the right thing for you.

Anxiety has been a part of my life since I was a young adult. However, it became heightened when I became a mother. And when I became a single mother, it consumed me. After years of working through my anxiety with counselling, meditation, yoga and the occasional diazepam, one day, this was not enough. Late one night, when I was suffering from insomnia, I experienced a wave of anxiety. During this, I imagined overdosing. My anxiety took over, and I feared that I was not in control of my body, which would theoretically lead to me accidentally overdosing. It turns out I was in control of my body, and I did not accidentally overdose, but it was this experience that made me realize I needed more help. I then started taking anti-depressants, which was the best decision I could have made. I now take 40mg of Citalopram every night and I'll happily admit that I couldn't have gotten through the last few years without them. Medication alone hasn't cured my anxiety, but it gave me the ability to think straight and not live in a constant state of panic. If you have never experienced anxiety before, this can be a terrifying time for you; I urge you to chat to your GP to discuss potential ways you can move forward. **Amy**

We advise you to speak to a qualified medical or psychiatric professional if you wish to explore medication for anxiety.

Choosing to take anti-anxiety medication is a valid choice. Some people worry that you will be judged badly for taking medication, especially as a parent. From our perspective, anyone who is doing what they can to overcome their challenges is doing something right. They are showing they recognize they have difficulties and they want to overcome them. This shows strength and bravery and insight and awareness, and this is all positive as a parent. Mental health difficulties such as anxiety exist. We cannot pretend otherwise. The important part is doing what you can to help yourself, and by doing so, helping your children.

While anxiety may feel like the end of the world right now, we are living proof that you can and will get through this.

Responding to Your Anxiety

Try this exercise the next time anxiety shows up. Take a deep breath, and then:

1. **Notice** when anxiety shows up for you. What are your own signs of anxiety showing up? Do you get restless? Do you feel your heart racing? Does your mind start jumping around?

2. **Acknowledge** this is anxiety (or any other emotions present you want to name). Acknowledge where you feel this in your body and how it wants you to behave. Acknowledge that anxiety shows up for you when you feel stressed, worried, overwhelmed, or tired.

3. **Reframe** your anxiety. Write down exactly what you are worried or anxious about. Make a note of all the worrying thoughts that have shown up. Go through the steps of checking out if there are any thinking errors or biases. Try to look at the situation from alternative perspectives; see if you can reframe the anxious thoughts to bring them to a fairer, calmer, more likely, less catastrophizing and more rational perspective. Remind yourself, "I am feeling anxious right now and my mind is sending me all sorts of anxious thoughts. I don't have to listen to them or

pay attention to them/believe in them, but I can recognize they are there."

4. **Problem-solve** by identifying the key worry or anxiety you are having and, once you have gone through the reframing process to bring it to a reasonable place, think about whether there is anything you need to do to address this worry. Keep an eye out for whether the "solution" involves any unhelpful anxiety behaviours (reassurance seeking, checking, avoiding); if it does, have a rethink about if you need to take action to solve the worry – or if what you need to do is to help calm and soothe yourself, as this may be the key problem-solving next step.

5. **Take action** to address the worry or anxiety if appropriate. Or take action to calm and soothe your body and mind. OR BOTH! Action to address the anxiety may take many forms: calming your thoughts, letting go of your thoughts, breathing exercises, applied relaxation, booking a therapy session, taking your medication, and/or doing some exercise.

6

DEPRESSION

Depression can be particularly prominent for single mothers. Indeed, this might be the chapter you've headed to straight away. The initial post-break-up of the family unit is a mentally draining period. Not simply because of the considerable shift in the family dynamic, but also often due to heartbreak, stress and overload. Depression can rear its head in various ways. You might lose your appetite, suffer from insomnia, feel empty, be unable to stop crying or perhaps feel unable to cry.

You might find that you're noticing what's going on around you more, your senses are heightened and you're suddenly aware of other families' dynamics – happy families seem to be all around you – and this is causing feelings of deep, deep sadness. It's a normal reaction to the trauma of a relationship breakdown, so don't feel bad if you have a sudden aversion to Tina, her sweet husband Kev and their irritatingly well-behaved little Alfie over there.

Amy experienced depression as a newly single mum, and struggled with seeing happy families. It took her a long time to not feel empty and heartbroken on seeing a simple family going about their business.

You might be feeling very low, but not sure if you have actual, diagnosable depression. How much sadness is normal? To be honest, labels don't matter as much as your experience. However, if you are sad to the point that you are finding it hard to function, seek help. If you are sad in a way that doesn't feel "normal" to you, seek help. If in doubt about your "level" of sadness, seek help.

Depression is a huge, complex subject in itself. In this chapter we'll look at how feelings of depression can manifest, and what we can do as single mums to alleviate very low feelings. The focus won't be on "solving" depression, but on understanding it, accepting your feelings and finding ways of coping that work for you.

WHAT IS DEPRESSION?

Depression is understood as an experience that can negatively affect how you feel, think and behave.

HOW CAN DEPRESSION MAKE YOU FEEL?

Depression can make you feel a range of emotions from sadness, distress, worry, guilt, anger, numbness, loneliness, anxiety, shame and so on.

Depression can also impact on how you feel physically. It can make you feel exhausted, physically and mentally fatigued, yet at the same time restless or agitated. It can make you feel like you are wading through treacle, as if every movement is hard. It can bring feelings of tension or a heaviness in chest and body.

HOW CAN DEPRESSION MAKE YOU THINK?

Depression can make you think you are a bad person, useless, a failure, not good enough. It can bring endless negative, critical and judgemental thoughts about you, your life, your past, your present, your future, others around you and the world. All those thinking biases we have been talking about in the previous chapters (see page 47) also have an impact here.

Depression can also impact on your cognition (for example, your attention, memory, speed of processing information). It can make it difficult to concentrate, remember things, to organize yourself, make decisions or problem-solve. It can feel like your brain is in a fog.

HOW CAN DEPRESSION MAKE YOU BEHAVE?

Depression can affect how you behave. It can make you want to withdraw, to hide away. It can make sleep impossible or become all-encompassing and you sleep too much. It can lead to tearfulness, agitation, rumination. You may neglect to take care of yourself, your wellbeing, food, health, self-care. It can trigger self-harm or suicidal behaviours (which we will talk about later in this chapter).

However, it is important to note that it is possible to function and have depression. It is possible to smile and laugh and have depression. It is possible to be a good friend to others, to look after yourself and your house, to outwardly appear like everything is "normal", and still have depression. You may be able to do all these things and then cry uncontrollably when a small thing happens or still feel overwhelmed, anxious, sad and broken inside. You may want to hide away, feel unable to face the day, feel shame, guilt, fear, struggle to sleep or get out of bed – but still appear the same old you to the outside world.

DEPRESSION ON A CONTINUUM VERSUS DEPRESSION AS A DIAGNOSIS

Do you have "depression"? What does depression look like? Unfortunately, depression does not have a particular "look" – it has many faces. Nevertheless, we can understand depression in two ways: as existing on a continuum, or as a specific diagnosis.

THE DEPRESSION SPECTRUM

People can have experiences of depression along a long continuum, ranging from not being depressed, to experiencing some minor depression symptoms, to having some severe depression symptoms, to being severely, all-encompassingly depressed. In this way, a person may move back and forward along the depression continuum, which might fluctuate over hours, days, weeks, with some moments seeming lighter and others feeling much, much heavier.

The idea of a depression spectrum can be helpful for single mothers who may wonder if they are depressed, but, because they have good days or good moments, think they can't be depressed. Within the spectrum, there is certainly space for all experiences of depression. This can then help us focus on finding ways to provide help and support, to move along the spectrum toward more and more days that fit under the experience of "not depressed".

In single motherhood, you may find yourself on any part of the depression continuum. If you have experienced depression in your life prior to becoming a single mother, you may be particularly susceptible to it rising up again at this time.

DEPRESSION AS A DIAGNOSIS

If depression is having an ongoing impact on your life, a formal diagnosis can be sought. This is not always needed, but at times can be helpful for you, or if the "system" requires a formal diagnosis; for example, to enable you to take sick leave or access medication or therapy services.

There are self-report questionnaires you can complete that can give an idea of your level of depression symptoms, and which indicate whether you may have a mild, moderate or severe level of depression. Depression can also be formally diagnosed by your doctor, psychiatrist or a suitably trained mental health professional.

Major depression (sometimes described as clinical depression) is the most common depression diagnosis. It is diagnosed according to specific criteria, and typically, symptoms have to be present for two weeks or more for a diagnosis to be made.

There are other mental health conditions that fit under the umbrella of depression diagnoses, which include: post-natal depression, seasonal affective disorder, depression with psychotic features or dysthymia. Bipolar Disorder (previously known as manic depression) is a related but very different condition, characterized by periods of mania (elevated mood and behaviours) and periods of depression.

In this chapter, we will talk about feelings of depression, which will encompass any experience along the depression continuum. This is important because you may experience depression symptoms in your journey of single motherhood without it ever reaching a "diagnosable/clinical" level, or you may experience ongoing depression that can impact on all areas of life and functioning, and which you may choose to seek a diagnosis and professional support for.

Remember, if you feel it would be helpful, professional support can always be explored, no matter how you understand the level of your depression experiences.

WHEN DEPRESSION CAN APPEAR IN SINGLE MOTHERHOOD

- When you are struggling with being alone, without a partner
- When you are struggling with the grief and losses you are experiencing in all areas of your life as a single mother
- When you are struggling to keep up with everything you have to do as a single parent

- When you are consumed with guilt, shame or regret about the journey to becoming a single mother
- When you are struggling with the shame and anxiety about being a single mother
- When you are struggling with the impact of single parenthood on your children
- When you cannot imagine your life getting to a better place
- When there are tough challenges – financial, practical, health – that you are struggling to overcome
- When there is ongoing conflict with your ex-partner or friends/family members related to the separation or life changes
- When you become overwhelmed with other life challenges, friendship breakdowns, bereavements, job losses

SELF-HARM AND SUICIDAL THOUGHTS

In the depths of depression, it is not uncommon to have suicidal thoughts or thoughts about harming yourself. If you are experiencing this, this is the point where we urge you to speak to your doctor or therapist if you already have one. I know this can be a scary topic to talk about, but it is also so, so important as the consequences of this part of depression can be devastating.

WHAT IS SELF-HARM?

Self-harm is a description for a set of behaviours that involve causing harm to the self. This may be through cutting, burning, scratching, hitting, picking. It can also be through excessive use of drugs, alcohol or food. These behaviours are not intended to cause harm to end a person's life, and so are not suicidal behaviours. Self-harm may occur as a way to:

- Numb feelings
- Create a sense of release from difficult emotions
- Feel something if you are feeling numb
- Inflict punishment through pain

Whatever the reason, it is an expression of the emotional pain a person is in, and the sense of the unbearable nature of this.

If self-harm has been or is a part of your life, there are ways to overcome this and develop new strategies for coping. Please seek help and support through a trained mental health professional to help you with this.

WHAT ARE SUICIDAL THOUGHTS?

There are different types of suicidal thoughts that people can experience.

- You may experience thoughts of wanting to end your life, of not wanting to be here anymore or wanting all the sadness or pain to stop.
- You may have thoughts of *actively* wanting to die.
- You may begin planning ways to cause your suicide – think about when and where you will do this.
- You may have thoughts justifying suicidal actions (for example, everyone will be better off without me).
- You may take steps toward your plans for suicide, such as write notes, buying medication.

Some people may experience only the first set of thoughts, but be very clear they do not want to act on them or ever do anything to cause their death. Thoughts like these still need and deserve support; but if the level and types of thoughts increase and escalate, it becomes crucial and, at times, urgent to seek help as soon as possible (see below).

It is important to understand that when we have thoughts of suicide it is our depressed brain trying to find a solution to the distress and pain you are feeling; the problem is it has got stuck on a faulty solution. The brain fails to tell you that suicide is *not* the only option – that this *will pass*, that people who have experienced suicidal thoughts can come through these and go on to live amazing incredibly lives. The brain is lying to us when it tells us everyone will be better off if we are not here – this is just NOT TRUE; especially for our children, but also for everyone else close to you to. Trying to recover from a loved one's suicide is a devastating experience.

WHAT TO DO ABOUT SUICIDAL THOUGHTS

- Talk to someone about how you're feeling.
- Call your national emotional support line (see Useful Resources).
- Contact your doctor.
- If you are already under the care of your local mental health team and they have a crisis line, call it.
- If you feel at risk of taking your own life, call the Emergency Services or go to the Emergency Room at your nearest hospital.

DO NOT GIVE UP if one of the options above doesn't help or isn't available. Try all and any of them. You are worth it.

STORIES OF DEPRESSION IN SINGLE MOTHERHOOD

Your life has completely turned upside down. You find yourself as a single parent and you are having to figure out a whole new way of being. Feelings of depression tend to appear when we feel life isn't going how we planned it, or feel that we have no control over what is happening to our lives. It can manifest in many different ways, but often you'll feel very low with little motivation to do anything, and it can feel like you are a shell of your former self.

*When **Ali** and her partner broke up, she felt defeated.*

"I was crying all the time, but I just kind of functioned. I had very little motivation, but, somehow, I managed to make sure my kids were always clean, fed and in a clean house. I, however, wouldn't have showered for days and would just be wearing joggers."

*When **Jemma's** marriage broke down, she soldiered on, despite an internal battle with depression.*

"When my marriage fell apart, I kept going. I had to. I worked. I kept the house tidy. I got the kids to school. I exercised (sometimes). I attended social events. I smiled. But inside I was struggling. I would cry in the car park on the way to the supermarket. I would feel overwhelmed by a text message that I needed to respond to or an email from school. I would find the kids' bedtime too much to cope with. I would wake early and just lie in bed thinking about everything that had happened, wanting to hide away and not face the day. But I had to earn, and I had to get up, and I had to keep going. At its worst, I had thoughts about whether I could continue, whether it would be easiest to not be here. Thankfully, those have passed now."

NEGATIVE FEELINGS ABOUT YOURSELF

It's a horrible feeling, not being wanted by someone that you loved so dearly. Even if you don't love them anymore, you might miss them but also start having doubts about yourself, like "What did I do wrong? What's wrong with me? Why don't they love me anymore?" Your relationship was a huge part of your life and, in a way, your sense of self, so when that gets shattered, you can be left with self-esteem issues and feeling extremely low in confidence. You might feel like you're unlovable or unattractive and that no one will want you. This is not the case, but it is a common way our minds can talk to us, especially the more that depression creeps in.

> **Kasia** thought she had found true love, the one person she wanted to be with for the rest of her life. Then it ended.
> "What dragged me down the most was that he was with me for so many years and then decided that he didn't want that anymore. It hurts that he saw me for me and didn't want to work on that. It's really hard to pick your self-esteem up from that without having any tools to help. It would have been so easy for me to spiral out of control, but for the sake of my daughter I just had to keep going and working on my depression with therapy and medication."

When you've been through a big break up, you can feel very down. We want you to know that you will get through this and you will find ways to boost your confidence back up. Unfortunately, low self-esteem and low confidence can eat you up inside and lead to feelings of depression.

> **Katie** struggled with thoughts about herself after the relationship breakdown.
> "Even though I agreed with the separation, it triggered a strong feeling of being rejected. I felt so rejected. I had

thoughts about not being cared for, that I didn't matter, that I wasn't worth anyone else's time. I was nothing. I noticed that this began to filter into my work and my time with my friends. If a situation at work became tricky I could view it as a rejection and a criticism of me. I became really sensitive to social group politics and to feeling left out. I realized, with support, that each of these situations was connecting to the thoughts of 'I am rejected' and 'I am not loved' and 'I don't matter'. That wasn't actually what was going on in those situations with work and friends, but that was how it was making me think and feel, and that would leave me feeling sad and hopeless and tearful and exhausted."

WHEN DEPRESSION AFFECTS YOUR FAMILY

Not only does depression affect yourself, but you might feel like it's causing issues within your family, particularly with your children.

*While **Ali** made sure her children were dressed, fed and watered each day, they still watched her struggle.*

"I think it impacted on my eldest the most because, for a long time, I just didn't find any pleasure in anything. He would say things like, 'Mummy, you just don't laugh anymore', and that broke my heart. There have been times where he's found me crying and given me a hug while I cry. Whereas my middle child would ask me why I'm crying, and I would tell him I was missing his daddy, and he would say things like, 'If I ask daddy, I think he would come home.'"

***Frankie** also felt there was a strain on her daughter.*

"When the depression got really bad, I was miserable to be around because everything was so much effort. I would try to put a face on for her, but there's no way they don't pick up on things."

When feelings of depression start affecting your family, that dreaded guilt loves to pop back in – as if we aren't feeling bad enough. You might be feeling guilty because you're too exhausted to do exciting things with your child, or guilty because you can't stop crying, or even because you just wish you could be the fun, peppy parent you thought you would be but are struggling so hard with right now. This is completely normal. See Chapter 4 for more on dealing with guilt.

If you are struggling with how you are feeling and it is something your children are witnessing, this can be an important time to seek extra help and support. Not because it is wrong for your children to see you have sad times, but because when it gets to the level where it is impacting you and your children, it is important to find ways to help all of you. And, while this is hard to hear, it will impact on your children if they have to care for you in your depression. So, even if you aren't feeling like you are worthy of this support right now, try to hold on to the fact it is worth it for your children and for the future you who will come through this and who deserves the chance to live a life without depression. Remember this can pass and get easier, so it is worth seeking support or help.

DEPRESSION AROUND CHILDREN

If you are experiencing depression, try to limit the burden your children may feel because of the depression, however old they are. Don't keep it inside or try to supress it, this isn't effective; but instead, try to talk about how you are feeling to others – friends, colleagues, family members. Contact a crisis text line and talk there.

Your mental health and wellbeing is a lot of responsibility for your child to hold and worry about, and if possible we want to spare them from this. This doesn't mean you have to only show them happy emotions, because this is not true or realistic. You can let them know you are having a sad moment, or a bad day, but it can help to spare them the details (particularly if it is related to their other parent).

TIPS FOR TALKING TO YOUR CHILD IF YOU ARE EXPERIENCING DEPRESSION AND LOW MOOD

- Tailor your conversation to their age: a six-year-old isn't going to understand the complexity of the situation like a teenager could.
- Be honest: answer their questions honestly, while being mindful of their age and emotional development.
- Make sure they understand that mental illnesses can't be caught, like Covid or a cold!
- Let them know you are struggling a bit or feeling a bit sad right now but also explain what you're doing to get better: talking to a doctor, taking medication, exercising, eating healthily, etc.

BEING ALONE

Parenting alone is tough. Especially when you're depressed, low and have no energy. Having another person to help makes it much easier, even if it's just for some moral support. Amy missed just being able to rant to someone about her day, but has found her friends have filled this gap. Luckily, one of her closest friends is a single parent too, so they have a daily Facetime routine where they check in on each other once their kids are asleep and just chat about their day. It's a chance to offload for both of them.

Ellie explains:

"I wish I had my child's dad to back me up with discipline sometimes, or someone to come home at the end of the day, or for someone to say you're doing a good job."

When things get really tough with the children, that lack of a partner can make things harder. It can be particularly tough to deal with major life problems and not have your partner to support you through them.

Amanda struggled with depression, not because she was alone, but because she was the only person dealing with her teenage son's depression and self-harming.

"I'm not saying it would have been easier to deal with my son's struggles if I had been in a healthy relationship, but just the idea of having someone to support me and help me through it might have stopped me from spiralling into depression myself."

When you don't have support from a partner, you need to find that support elsewhere, whether it's through going to therapy, asking a friend or family member or joining a support group for single parents. Just because you are single does not mean you have to do this alone. There are people out there that can help you. If you're feeling depressed, even if you don't want to, we urge you to talk to someone, even if it's just a friend, colleague or neighbour – someone that can support you or offer a hand when things are getting really tough.

When Frankie was having really bad days her best friend would come over, play with her daughter and give her a cup of tea.

"I could not have got through that period without her, and I think my daughter would have suffered more if she hadn't stepped in and given her all that attention."

We all love to think we can do things on our own, and we might even feel like we need to prove to people that we are fine and can manage as single parents. There can be a lot of pressure after a relationship breakdown, but in reality, we need to be able to ask for help. That is the strongest thing you can do for yourself and your children when you are struggling with your mental health.

Frankie's *top advice:*

"If your friends want to help you, then let them! They're offering because they want to, not because they feel like they have to. It took me a while to realize those offers are genuine. Your children won't be permanently damaged from this break-up, they will grow up feeling loved and taken care of because of what you will do. You can only control yourself and your actions, and just give yourself and your kids as much love and support as possible and you will get through it. It will be shit, but it will get better."

SELF-HARM AND SUICIDAL THOUGHTS

Although this section was a particularly difficult one to write, we want to make sure no single mother feels suicide is the only way out. Tragically, Amy has personal experience of a friend's suicide; she was a single mother and, devastatingly, her children were the ones to find her. While this is incredibly upsetting to discuss, we hope that by talking about depression, self-harm and suicidal thoughts, we will encourage anyone experiencing these feelings to seek help – if not for yourself, then for your children, your family and your friends.

> *I went through a depressive stage about a year after my ex and I broke up. I've touched upon it in the anxiety chapter but to summarize, it was the middle of the night and I was so anxious that I believed I was not in control of my body and that I would accidentally take an overdose, leaving my son to find me. I didn't sleep that night and instead booked a doctor's appointment first thing in the morning. My doctor was extremely comforting and helped me differentiate between these intrusive thoughts and reality. I started anti-depressants that day and they completely changed my life. **Amy***

Experiencing suicidal thoughts as a single mother can be really scary. Amy's came in the form of an anxious intrusive thought. For others it may be through specific negative thoughts or images.

> As **Allison's** relationship was breaking down, she also had to go through the pain of losing her mum. When her mum passed away, she felt like she couldn't cope anymore at all.
> *"I felt completely alone. I seriously thought my kids would be better off if I wasn't there; I knew that they would go and live with their grandparents, and I thought that would be easier. I felt like that for about a week, then I seriously considered driving my car off the bridge. I nearly did it, but something stopped me, and I drove straight to the doctors and talked to them. They gave me sleeping tablets, started me on anti-depressants straight away and I started therapy soon after."*

Often, the thought of our children having to go on through life without us will stop us from actually acting on suicidal thoughts.

For example, single mum Ellie would drive with her daughter's teddy in the back seat to remind her that she needed to drive straight home because she was waiting for her, and she couldn't let her down.

While Allison and Ellie managed to bring themselves out of their suicidal thoughts, many people do not receive the care they need. If you are struggling, we urge you now to reach out for help.

UNHEALTHY COPING HABITS

We all have different coping methods, but it is all too easy to fall into unhealthy coping habits. Many of us indulge in a glass of wine after a hard day, or a cigarette to take the stress off; but when we feel very low and depressed we might turn to these habits even more, to numb, to feel and to cope.

*When **Allison's** relationship with her husband broke down, she started drinking too much and isolating herself. It was at this point she decided to change her friendship group, because she didn't want to see all of her old friends who also knew her husband.*

"I got into a cycle of drinking alcohol and barely leaving the house. I downloaded the Bumble friends app, and met my now best friend; she helps to bring me out of depressive states by forcing me on walks, or she looks after my children so I can rest. I also took up some new hobbies, so I didn't have to think about the mess of my life at the time."

Finding healthy ways to bring yourself out of low moods can be tough but so important. It's so easy to self-medicate with booze, drugs, cigarettes, unhealthy eating habits, overworking, or by being overly controlling. While it's okay to let your hair down and do what you need to do to get through each day, it's important to also incorporate healthy coping methods into your routine, which hopefully outweigh the unhealthy ones!

SOME HEALTHY COPING METHODS

- Socialize – reach out to your friends or family.
- Exercise – we know, we know, we're always told to, but seriously, it helps!
- Eat well – don't skip meals and try your hardest to eat some healthy meals.
- Dance – stick on some music and just go with it.
- Sleep – if you're struggling, have a chat with your doctor to discuss how you can improve this.
- Do yoga – it's relaxation and exercise all in one!
- Do things for you – go to the hairdressers, buy that dress you like, do things that make you feel good.
- Clean your house – for some, their mental state is so much worse when their house is a mess.
- Journal – write about your day and keep track of what has made you happy or sad each day.
- Have a digital detox – stay away from your devices for a couple of hours.

The above list provides seemingly simple lifestyle coping methods, but it is important to realize that making small changes in life can make big changes to your mind. Ask yourself which of the above methods (or others if you can think of them) could work for you, and do one of those things today. Done it? Then let's try another tomorrow. All we need to do is take it one day at a time.

WAYS TO HELP YOURSELF THROUGH DEPRESSION

There are different strategies, activities and approaches we can use to help ourselves when we are feeling caught up in depression. We have shared a number of ideas and techniques which you can use to help you. As with the advice in the other chapters, there is no one set way to find your way out of depression. The most important thing is to find the ways that work for you.

ESTABLISH A ROUTINE

Even in the depths of depression there are small things you should try to do each day; they might seem obvious, but in the darkest days it's easy to give up on yourself. So, each day try to:

- Brush your teeth
- Wash your face
- Brush your hair
- Have a shower or bath
- Get changed out of your pyjamas – even if it's just to put fresh pyjamas on

It can help to create a simple routine that you stick to each day. Then, even if you're feeling so down and can't think straight, you can automatically do what you need to do each day. For example, every morning Amy gets her son's clothes out and makes his breakfast. While he's eating, Amy will have a coffee and get dressed. Then she gets him dressed, teeth brushed, and then they're off to school. These are all basic things that might seem like standard when you're feeling mentally well, but when your brain is not playing ball, even the simplest things can feel like climbing a mountain.

DON'T WAIT TO FEEL BETTER BEFORE YOU START DOING

It is easy to feel like you don't have the motivation to do anything when you feel depressed. However, if we wait for the motivation to appear we might be waiting a long time as the depression can make motivation sink lower and lower. So while it is important to allow yourself rest and to listen to your body when you need to sit on the sofa and watch a movie rather than be "doing", it is also important to know when to encourage yourself to get up and do, even if you don't feel like it, in order to regain your motivation. When we do activities that will benefit us (for example, seeing friends, getting tasks done, exercising) our mood and motivation improve, and each time it will get a little easier.

DO THINGS THAT YOU ENJOY OR BRING YOU A SENSE OF ACHIEVEMENT

There is a therapeutic approach called Behavioural Activation, which is based on the premise that, to build our mood up, we need to do more of the things that helps us feel good, either through enjoyment or through the sense of achievement. When we withdraw and avoid doing things in depression, we lose a source of positive reinforcement. So take some time to think about the things that you enjoy (or used to enjoy before the depression).

Is there anything you have stopped doing that you can restart? What can you plan for that you know you will enjoy? It could be simply watching your favourite film or TV show, cooking your favourite meal, spending time with friends, doing a hobby, taking part in your favourite sport, going to see live music, and so on; or it could be tackling some annoying tasks that have been lingering on your to-do list, sorting through some jobs in the house, completing some DIY or other aspects of general life administration; it could even be completing a training course for work.

Whatever you choose, it is important to do these things one step at a time, in manageable chunks. But do something.

EXERCISE

Setting yourself an active goal and working slowly toward it, can bring an amazing feeling of achievement. Exercise can be anything that works for you: running, hiking, climbing, swimming, paddleboarding, dance, yoga, Pilates, boxing, cycling, rowing, spinning, HIIT workouts, walking – ANYTHING that gets you moving more.

And exercising outside provides an added bonus, as being in nature, fresh air and sunlight can further benefit our mental health. So, even on the most difficult days, trying to get outside for a walk can be really helpful – even if you just go round the block or round the garden. You can also try enlisting a friend or family member to stay active with you, which can help on the days you really don't feel like doing anything.

THE PSYCHOLOGICAL BENEFITS OF EXERCISE

Exercise is so good for our mental health in all ways, and depression is no exception. Research studies have found exercise to have anti-depressant effects on our mental health. Exercise has also been found to improve sleep, confidence, energy levels, self-esteem, decision-making, problem-solving, memory, concentration, motivation and much more.

STAY SOCIAL

Social interaction has been demonstrated to help when we are feeling low. The instinct in depression is to withdraw and stay away from people. However, spending time with others is proven to lift our mood – no matter the size of group: perhaps one-to-one to start with and larger groups when you're ready. No matter what your mind tries to convince you, don't shut people out. Being around people helps because it provides you with the opportunity to talk to others about how you are, and you can also talk about them. Depression tends to pull our focus inwards to ourselves, so it can be helpful and healthy to focus on others too.

TACKLE YOUR THOUGHTS

Depression can be driven by some very negative powerful, critical thoughts that might swirl around your mind day and night. So, we need to tackle these thoughts. If we change the thoughts or how we respond to the thoughts, we can begin to change how we are feeling.

As we have talked about with anger and anxiety, it is really important to mindfully notice the thoughts your mind is sending you when you are feeling depression, and say to yourself, "I am noticing I am having the thought that ..." (for example, "I notice I am having the thought that no one cares about me").

Remind yourself that just because these thoughts are there, it does not mean they are true. Notice if there are any of those unhelpful thinking patterns or biases in your thoughts (black and white thinking, mindreading, emotional reasoning, jumping to conclusions, etc).

Remind yourself that, just because these thoughts are there, you don't have to believe them or let them control you or your behaviour. It is likely that there is a fairer and more reasonable and kinder thought that you could hold on to instead; ask yourself, "What would I say to a friend if they told me they were thinking these things?" You could also say to yourself, "Oh my mind is being really mean/unkind today. It is being really bullying, but I don't have to listen to it or give it my attention."

You can treat your thoughts like a radio in the background – these thoughts can rumble on in the background, like a radio tuned to negative FM, but you don't have to give the radio channel much of your attention. Or you can imagine these thoughts in silly ways – imagine them being spoken in a Mickey Mouse voice, sung by an opera singer or to the tune of happy birthday. Or simply talk to yourself kindly, gently and with compassion – an antidote to the negative thoughts.

Another good way to tackle your thoughts is by journaling. Spend some time each day to get all your thoughts out of your head and onto paper, as this can help you feel more able to cope with them.

LOOK AFTER YOURSELF

Looking after yourself is an essential part of any day, but with depression the simple things can be even harder. Looking after yourself can mean taking care to wash, dress nicely, feed yourself. It can also mean taking time for nicer self-care activities: a warm bath, a favourite movie, a massage, a pamper session, an early night. Anything that makes you feel calm, soothed and cared for. You deserve that, and it is an important part of looking after yourself as you come through experiences of depression.

ACCEPT HELP

It is really important to accept help when you are struggling. It can be easy to want to show you can cope, and as a single mum you might feel that pressure even more so. You might always not want to accept help as you don't want help with childcare or life admin, or with anything else.

THERAPY

Therapy can be a lifeline – regardless of depression. If we all just had some time to sit down with someone and dissect our thoughts and feelings, perhaps we would be leading much happier, healthier lives. Not only can therapy help you to figure out what's causing your feelings of depression and what you can do to combat it, but it can help you examine other situations in your life that you might not have realized were triggering.

For depression, many approaches can be helpful, including CBT, ACT and EMDR, which we have discussed earlier. In addition to these approaches are Compassion-focused Therapy (CFT) and Psychodynamic psychotherapy. As with ACT and CBT, Compassion-focused Therapy offers ways of understanding your experiences and developing new ways of responding to your thoughts, feelings and behaviours. Psychodynamic psychotherapy can be short- or long-term therapy. This therapy approach can focus on unconscious processes, internal conflicts and relationship dynamics.

The best therapy approach may depend on what fits best with you and what is underlying your depression. And if you have tried something before that didn't work for you, don't give up – try a different approach. We recommend you seek out a clinical or counselling psychologist or psychotherapist who may have a range of skills and therapy approaches that they can tailor to suit you. However, you may also find it helpful talking to a counsellor to have the space to talk through everything that is happening for you.

It might feel daunting deciding to go for therapy, and you might not know exactly how you can access therapy. Your doctor should be able to direct you to the free services available, although there can be significant waiting lists; and paying for private therapy can be costly. Always check the qualifications of the therapist you would like to see and, where appropriate, make sure they have the training and qualifications you need and that they are registered with a professional body.

A big part of therapy success is forming a positive relationship with the therapist you are working with. You must feel able to trust them and feel safe working with them. Therapy can be tough and challenging, but doing the work in therapy can be hugely rewarding.

Although meeting a person for therapy is an ideal solution, there is also guided self-help, which has many positives, such as being free and can fit around a busy schedule. Guided self-help materials can help you work through how you are thinking and feeling and help you find new ways of coping. It can also be helpful to read about others' experiences of depression, and there are also some great mental health-based podcasts that could help. We have included a selection of our favourites in the Useful Resources.

*After **Ali's** relationship broke down, therapy helped her to realize some truths about her relationship.*

"I learnt from therapy that my relationship was extremely toxic, and that my reaction to the emotional abuse is referred to as trauma bonding. No matter how badly my ex treated me, I would always want to talk to him, which was causing more and more harm each time. I'm in a better position now thanks to lots of therapy, and have been working on having no contact with my ex (my mum does the communication regarding the children); the longer I go without speaking to him, the better I feel."

***Sam** has suffered with anxiety and depression for a long time, and decided to seek counselling in a bid to save her marriage. When that didn't work, she continued with therapy.*

"Therapy has been my saviour. I now allow the feelings to flow when they need to, but without being consumed by them. It's a rollercoaster, but it feels healthy. Some days are meant to be sad, others happy. I would definitely suggest therapy to anyone and everyone!"

MEDICATION

Despite the growing number of people seeking help for depression, there still seems to be an embarrassment around taking anti-depressants. Choosing to go on medication is a very personal choice. For Amy, while she didn't like the idea of going to the doctors and telling them she was struggling in case they thought she couldn't look after her son, it was actually the best decision she ever made. While medication didn't cure her depression, it helped Amy cope and gave her the options to work on herself in other ways. Of course, anti-depressants won't be the right solution for everyone, but if you are wondering if it might be for you, open up a conversation with your family doctor to discuss what you can do next.

Frenchie *started anti-depressants after becoming a single mum.*

"I feel a lot more active now. It took me a long time to come to terms with my depression, and a long time to 'give up' (which is what it felt like at the time) and go on to meds. I don't know why I was so against them. I was having stress-related chest pains that would freak me out enough to need to go to the Emergency Room."

It can be scary to feel like you're "giving in" to anti-depressants, but you need to be willing to adjust your mental health plan to suit you, and that might be medication. Only you and your doctor or qualified mental health professional can work out what is the best route for you.

Kasia has been on some form of anti-depressants for the last ten years. However, since moving into a house on her own, she's been taking them every day.

"Before, I would sometimes not take them to see what happened. However, now I completely avoid that self-destructive behaviour. I think it's because my daughter is no longer a baby, and I don't want to risk her seeing me so sad all the time."

When we can feel self-destructive behaviour creeping in – such as not taking our medication – it's important to find ways to overcome these unhelpful behaviours either working out ways to do this ourselves or with professional support.

REMEMBER SELF-COMPASSION

Okay, so you're having mental health issues – STOP JUDGING YOURSELF RIGHT NOW. Mental health problems are very common, and the last thing your brain needs right now is you beating yourself up about something you were unable to prevent. Now is the time to look after yourself, practise self-care and give yourself time to heal.

Our minds in depression tend to be incredibly self-critical. Talking kindly and compassionately to ourselves can make a huge difference. Try these kinder words:

- Instead of "I'm such a failure", try "I am doing my best at a really hard time".
- Instead of "I'm a terrible mum", try "I am a good mum who wants the best for my children. There is only so much I can do at any one time. I am only one person and only human".
- Instead of "No one loves me", try "I am loved. I have friends and family who care. Right now I miss having a partner, and that is really hard; but I can explore new relationships in the future when I am ready".

Mental health conditions are as serious as physical health illnesses, so we should be treating them as such. You wouldn't tell someone with a broken leg to ignore the pain and go for a run, so why should someone with depression feel like they should ignore their sadness and power on through. It's a recipe for serious breakdown, and one that can be avoided with the proper mental health care, support and guidance.

IT WILL GET EASIER

We promise – it will get easier! It may get harder before it gets easier, but if you give yourself some time, you will get through this. As you start working on yourself and giving your brain that TLC it so desperately craves, you'll become more equipped to deal with low moods as they arise. You just need to take it one day at a time.

Kelly agrees:

"The bad days don't last forever. I got good at predicting when they were coming and so expected less of myself or just kind of let them happen, knowing that I would come out of them (as I had before)."

7 SMALL STEPS TO HELP YOU RIGHT NOW

1. Kind self-talk: Notice how you are talking to yourself. Say something kind and compassionate to yourself right now, as if you were talking to a friend. Let yourself know this is hard, and you deserve kindness not criticism.

2. Take a moment and take three slow, deep, calming breaths; slowly soothingly, tell yourself "This is tough, but I can get through this."

3. Think about how you are looking after yourself right now. Are you eating, washing, taking care of your home? Choose one nice thing to do for yourself – and do it today.

4. Have you stepped outside today? How much have you moved today? Take a quick walk outside or round the garden; if you can't leave the house, do some stretching or try an online yoga class. Try and move a little today, even if you don't feel like it.

5. Consider if there is someone you can reach out to today. Have a look through your phone, and choose someone to say hi to, have a chat with, organize a coffee with, to say "I'm struggling a bit today." You deserve love and support.

6. Consider if there is anything – hobbies, interests, plans, activities – that you have stopped doing because of the way you feel. Choose something you think you could slowly restart and make a plan today. Even if you don't feel like it, give this a go.

7. Lastly, find some music on your phone, on your Alexa, on the radio. Find a song you love and which makes you feel strong, determined, brave – that makes you want to keep going, feel empowered, energized. Blast this out loud (or on your headphones!) right now.

PART TWO

MOVING FORWARD

7

FROM POWERLESS TO POWERFUL

The experience of becoming a single mother can leave you feeling in a very vulnerable position. From being unable to change the situation that has led you to become a single mother, to dealing with finances, to losing the freedoms a two-adult household provided, there are many reasons why you may be feeling powerless right now. In this chapter we're going to explore this feeling of powerlessness and discover practical steps to finding our power again.

WHAT DO WE MEAN BY "POWERLESS" AND "POWERFUL"?

Powerlessness often refers to the sense of having no influence over, or ability to determine, the outcomes you seek. If you feel powerless, you may believe you do not have the power to control how you want things to be in your life. A sense of powerlessness can make us feel anxious, fearful, sad, scared, worried, angry, frustrated and overwhelmed.

In contrast, when we feel powerful, we believe we have control over and an impact on how our life can be or how events will be. A sense of being powerful can make us feel strong, confident, secure and positive about the future.

It is important to note, however, that we can find our power without necessarily feeling "all" powerful. Whilst feeling you have power in your life and a sense of being powerful rather than powerless can be a positive thing, power can be harnessed in unhealthy ways. You may be familiar with this when you are made to feel powerless by someone who is wielding all the power, or when you may be tempted to exert your power and control resulting in someone else feeling powerless. This challenging dynamic is often present in relationship breakdowns, where the notion of power and who has the power can be an area of conflict. Power can also be exerted through societal views and systems which may leave you feeling powerless. We will explore this more through this chapter.

WHEN MIGHT YOU FEEL POWERLESS IN SINGLE MOTHERHOOD?

- When you are unable to stop the situation that leads you into single motherhood (whether this is because a partner passes away or because they leave).
- When you realize you are on your own (and for the moment there is no other option).
- When you lose your sense of identity as a family/ being married/part of a couple, and cannot (at this time) reverse this.
- When you know you cannot heal your children's hurt by giving your children the family they miss or may want (both their parents together).
- When you feel you have no control over situations involving your ex-partner, such as how they communicate or behave, or when they introduce your child to a new partner.

- When you feel unable to improve your career, fitness or financial situation due to childcare responsibilities or practical restrictions.
- When you don't like your ex-partner's new partner or extended family or friends, and/or don't think they treat your child well but you have no power to stop them being around them.

WHEN POWER AND CONTROL IS MISUSED

It can become easy in the anger and conflict that arises in the breakdown of a relationship for power and control to be misused, leaving one person holding a lot of power and the other feeling incredibly powerless. The dynamic between two separated partners who may struggle to communicate, and who have their own (different) perceptions of the situation, their own anger, grief, rage, sadness, shame, can easily be misdirected into an abuse of the power dynamic. We might see this abuse of power and control in:

- How much one parent has access to the children or contact with them
- Financial arrangements or distribution of previous shared belongings
- What one parent is allowed to say to or do with the children
- Refusing to be flexible for one-off events; for example, change in drop-off time, extra childcare cover, holidays, access for special occasions

Even in amicable separations, it can be easy to be drawn into a tit-for-tat power play: "You've hurt me/been unhelpful, so I will hurt you/be unhelpful too."

In the worst of situations, this power and control is achieved through threats of withdrawal of finances, time with the children, communication or, sadly, through threats or actual verbal or physical abuse.

Ultimately, when control and power is misused repeatedly in this way, it is abuse, whether that is emotional, verbal or physical. This abuse may have been present in the relationship before, or it may have developed during the conflict of the separation – whichever, it is unacceptable.

If you are being placed in a powerless position because of this type of behaviour, please reach out for help. If you are experiencing any type of abuse, please reach out for help. We know this will be hard, but help is out there. And if you find yourself engaging in this kind of behaviour – causing someone else to feel powerless – please also reach out for help.

Your options may include:

- Seeing a therapist for yourself, for support, and to understand and find ways to cope with what is happening. Finding a therapist who works with relationships, even if you are seeing them alone, can be helpful.
- If you are concerned about the children, you can seek advice about safeguarding with your local government child welfare services (e.g. Social Services team in the UK), and you can do this anonymously. We know this may feel like a scary thing to do, but they will work with you to ensure the children are safe and cared for. They also often have training courses, advice and support for parents and families.

- You can contact organizations dedicated to supporting couples, families, or anyone in a situation of abuse. See Useful Resources for a list of these.
- If you (or those around you) are at immediate risk or in danger, please call the police.

STORIES OF POWERLESSNESS AND POWER IN SINGLE MOTHERHOOD

REALIZING YOU'RE ON YOUR OWN

There are going to be so many times within our lives where we feel powerless. However, one that sticks into most single mothers' minds is when we first realize that we're on our own and there is nothing (at this time) that we can do about that. It can be very daunting not having the back-up of a partner while you're parenting.

> **Allison** explains the moment it hit her that she was now on her own.
>
> "I took my newborn baby with me to collect my two-year-old from nursery. He was tired, and did the classic thing of screaming and shouting that he doesn't want to come home with me. So, I was lugging a baby and an angry toddler home with me and that's when I realized, I was completely on my own in this."

While in some situations the single mother may feel relieved to be doing this alone, without any tension or disagreements, others will find it extremely overwhelming. And the constant reminders from a small human don't help:

"Why is daddy not here anymore?"

"Will daddy come back? I want daddy to come back."

There was absolutely nothing I could do to sew our little family back together again. My son's father didn't love me anymore, but no amount of explaining the complex world of love to a four-year-old could make it any better. It was completely out of my control, and I don't think I've ever felt so powerless in a situation. **Amy**

Ishana found herself a single mother at 25 when her daughter's father was unable to commit to consistent care due to his own alcohol addiction issues.

"I had never wanted to have a child on my own, but from the pregnancy onward, my daughter's dad wasn't reliable. He would miss appointments and not come home, or be too drunk, or spend our money. I quickly realized I had to protect my daughter and myself from this, and we found our own place. It was heartbreaking, as I desperately wanted him to be okay and get help and be a good dad. Over the years, I've tried to involve him in our daughter's life, but each time he's let us both down. I felt powerless to help with his addiction and powerless to give my daughter the family or father she deserved."

Roxy met her children's dad when they were young, and after separating he went on to marry and have another child, and his new partner actively discouraged his involvement with them.

"Ten years in, their father has become less and less involved. He hardly ever sees them, and so now the overriding feelings are powerlessness for being unable to fix this for the children – who are so aware of their dad's lack of interest – and utter guilt for not choosing a better partner to have children with."

WHEN YOU HAVE TO RELINQUISH CONTROL

There's a feeling of lack of control around so many aspects of parenting. It's not always about the lack of control related to an ex-partner, it could be due to legal situation – if you're going through a divorce or have a Child Arrangement Order from the family court, you might feel like you're having decisions taken away from you, and that can really impact your mental health and make you feel vulnerable and powerless.

Allison explains how court-ordered visitation can cause her more emotions than expected.

"I have a court order in place for my children going to their dad's house. However, I feel awful when my youngest cries his eyes out and tells me he doesn't want to go, but there's nothing I can do about it. I like the freedom it gives me, and I am so grateful that they do go, but when he is so upset, I just want to keep him home."

Bethany became a single mum in her early 30s. As the separation went on her ex-boyfriend became more controlling, despite him having found someone new. He would question her career choices, how she looked after the house, and he would tell her how to do things. He would email or message her many times a day. He would withhold funds or his attention or time with the children if Bethany argued with him. Bethany's mental health deteriorated and she felt more and more controlled, distressed, angry and powerless.

"I knew his behaviour wasn't okay and yet I also wanted to do whatever I could to keep him happy and keep the peace so he wouldn't take it out on me or the children. And I would feel terrible, like it was my fault for not being better at making things okay."

Bethany's experience is an extreme one, yet sadly not necessarily uncommon. It is also emotionally controlling and abusive – and NOT okay. If you are in this situation please do reach out for help and support.

CHILDREN BEING INTRODUCED TO A NEW PARTNER

An area you might feel powerless to do anything about is when your child is introduced to your ex's new partner and/ or family/kids.

> *I was absolutely devastated when I found out my son had been introduced to a new woman without my agreement. Hearing about their days out from my child made me feel like I was being replaced. When, in reality, no one could ever replace me! I'm that kid's mother, and I'm a damn good one!*
>
> *My son's dad had an agreement with me that he would tell me before my son had a sleepover at his girlfriend's house. After picking up my child one day he told me that "the sleepover went well". Here, I saw red. Having absolutely no power over where my son had spent the night induced the ol' rage machine inside of me. I had never met his girlfriend and didn't even know where she lived, so the thought of my son staying at a house with people I don't know in a place I don't know made me feel physically sick. The fact that this happened without my knowledge made me lose trust in my ex-partner and fractured our co-parenting relationship. However, I now realize that the more people in my child's life that love him and care for him, the better.* **Amy**

Frankie *summarizes it perfectly:*

"While it isn't always easy to know there is another woman involved in my daughter's life in a parental way, if they get along and she loves her, that is the most important part. Her being surrounded by people who love her is more important than all of our egos. When I want to respond immediately to a difficult situation with my ex, I always remind myself, our daughter being happy is the most important thing."

Katie's *experience of this process went somewhat more smoothly, but still left her feeling very powerless.*

"My ex-partner and I had a fairly amicable relationship, and he let me know about his new girlfriend fairly early on. We both agreed the children didn't need to be involved until it was more serious. After a few months he began to talk about her meeting the children. We planned for me to meet his new girlfriend first, which went well; but we disagreed about the timing for the children. Luckily we kept communicating around it, and I was fortunate that he did delay in line with my wishes. In this instance, for a while, I did have some power, which made things easier. After a few more months, I agreed he could go ahead and introduce them. I did feel very powerless at knowing I couldn't put it off forever, and that I couldn't be there for them or to talk to them about it in advance because their dad would do that. I hated knowing this was a situation they had to face. In the end it went okay, although the children did, and still do, feel sad about the situation, and say it makes them feel 'funny' inside. All I can do is try to give them space to talk and help them through how they are feeling."

BRING BACK THE POWER

*"The most common way people give up their power is
by thinking they don't have any."*

Alice Walker, Author

So, what can we do to try and assert some power and control
back into our lives? Firstly, there are day-to-day things we can
do to help us feel we have power and control over our new
lives, our new solo-parent identity; secondly, we can focus on
specific psychological strategies to help us regain a sense of
power with how we choose to think, feel and act in certain
challenging scenarios.

FINDING POWER IN YOUR NEW LIFE

There are some practical things you can do day to day that will
help you feel like you are more in control of your life and living
the life you want. Take time to try different and new things (habits,
routines, traditions) to find out what works for you and your
children in this new life of single motherhood. This is about finding
you and who you are and what works for your new family set-up.

It can be very empowering to get your finances into order. By
creating spreadsheets of all incomings and outgoings for every
month, you can make sure you have enough money to pay the
bills each month.

Find the confidence to say yes to social situations. By doing
this you could end up doing a whole load of new things you
might not have done before – such as going to gigs, day trips
out and random dates!

If a career is important to you, then focus on that. You may
find satisfaction and a sense of achievement from focusing on
your progress here.

Prioritize looking after yourself. Whether it is taking the time for a new skincare regime, hair appointment, exercising, eating well, choosing some new clothes or blasting your favourite music, looking after yourself sends the message to yourself that you matter, that you deserve care, that you are in control of looking after yourself and your life. It helps you hold your head up even higher.

It may sound a bit like a cliché, but redecorating can be a quick win in regaining some control for newly single mums – there's no one to argue with about paint colours, so long as the children are happy to go along with it. While a full-on renovation isn't always feasible, there are always smaller things you can do to change things up – move the furniture around, put up pictures of your friends and family. Or you could always use your newfound freedom to brush up on your DIY skills.

When **Tegan** moved out, she turned into a house-renovating goddess.

"I've decorated from top to bottom: stripped wallpaper, sanded, painted, put up shelves and mirrors, re-pressurized the boiler (that does feel good, really good) and managed to work out the boiler programme on the thermostat, set up all the gadgets, made the flatpack furniture on my own, and stripped back the jungle of a garden. Also, I felt absolutely no shame in getting help when needed. I've made a home!"

Francesca's ex-partners were terrible with DIY and she absolutely loves that she's determined to get things done.

"Being able to jumpstart my ex's car using some cables was a real highlight for me – I've never felt so powerful!"

FINDING POWER THROUGH LIVING LIFE BY YOUR VALUES

Finding meaning in our lives and living meaningful lives, even in challenging situations, can be helped by living life according to your values.

Acceptance and Commitment Therapy explains how values are like a compass that help show you which way to go, how to behave, who you want to be. Values may include any of the following (and there are many more):

- Courage
- Forgiveness
- Fun
- Honesty
- Compassion
- Connection
- Patience
- Self-control
- Responsibility
- Kindness
- Respect
- Independence

The concept of living by your values means that, even when you encounter hard times (such as the challenge of a relationship breakdown and becoming a single mother), rather than getting lost in conflict, emotion or overwhelming thoughts about the situation, you instead focus on how you want to be as a single mother. What values are important to you in the person you are and in the way you want to live your life? How can you let these values guide you, act as your compass, steer you toward a meaningful life, no matter how challenging life becomes? Values are different to goals, and can be lived even when your life goals change. Finding power through your values could mean living life with compassion, forgiveness, fun, courage, independence and connection. Imagine being able to draw on all these values in how you live day to day. How would this feel? Build your power through living the values that are meaningful to you.

FINDING POWER THROUGH ASSERTIVENESS

Becoming a single mum means suddenly everything is on you. Decisions, negotiations, communicating with everyone – from the gas man to your children's school to social situations. It's just you. Which can be really blooming scary sometimes. When we feel powerless we can feel like we have lost our voice, so developing the ability to be assertive and speak up for yourself can be an incredibly powerful skill; whether it be with a sales person, your partner, when you begin dating, or anything else.

Assertiveness is the ability to clearly communicate how you think and feel, standing up for your own needs/rights or the needs/rights of others, without reverting to passive aggressive or aggressive communication styles. When you are assertive, you must always keep in mind the person you are communicating with and respect their thoughts and feelings. Being assertive isn't about getting your way or holding power over someone else, it is about owning and clearly communicating your thoughts and feelings and being able to listen to someone else's thoughts and feelings too. As such, it also provides an effective way for concerns or difficulties to be addressed without it becoming a conflict. At times, however, it will be about assertively setting out your boundaries and knowing for yourself whether there is any wriggle room on these.

You can focus on developing your assertiveness skills in the following ways:

- Practise – it won't always come easily or naturally, so just keep having a go and you will find it becomes more natural with practice.

- Sit with discomfort – If you aren't naturally assertive, you will have to tolerate a certain amount of discomfort as you get used to it.
- Focus on asking for what you need when you need it, using simple language, and be open to being flexible and negotiating where appropriate.
- Focus on owning what you are saying, "I would like …", "I feel …".
- Notice your language and know that you can be assertive, calm and kind and compassionate in your communication.
- Aim to communicate calmly and respectfully, keep an eye on your tone and body language alongside what you are saying.
- Be open to a discussion and listening to the other person.
- If you are saying no, and hate having to say no to people, it may well take time and practice. For example, you could say, "I'm sorry that won't work for me, but you go ahead" or "I'm not available, but thank you for asking".

FINDING POWER IN YOUR RELATIONSHIP WITH YOUR EX

Learn what works best for you with regards to contact with your ex-partner. Instead of freaking out about things you can't control, try to reframe your attitude toward them – remember, you *are* in control of how you react and cope with these situations.

For some, this might be to minimize contact; this can be hard because you have a child together or if you have been together for a long time, but it is important to do this if the contact you do have makes you feel unempowered. Others might feel empowered by improving the communication with their ex, and developing a calmer, civil, mature relationship. The important thing is there is no right or wrong way, it is just about discovering what helps you feel empowered rather than powerless and going with that, *while being mindful not to make your ex-partner powerless in the process.*

If you have a court-ordered agreement, you need to stick to it even if the kids don't want to go that day. To regain the power from this situation, focus on what you have power over rather than what you don't. Try to plan something for yourself on those days – something that will make you feel good and happy. It could be meeting up with friends, getting your nails done, or going to watch a movie you can't see when you've got the children. This time is yours and you deserve this break.

Hard as it may be, it's worth trying to see your ex introducing a new partner as a positive – it is, after all, one more person in your child's life to care for them.

You can exert some control over this situation by asking your ex to talk to you before they introduce your kids to a new partner; you could even ask to meet the new partner first. At the very minimum, it's definitely worth finding out the name of the new partner so you can normalize the idea of a new partner for your kids' sake. While your ex may say no or completely disregard your agreements in the future, by making these simple requests you have done what you can to ensure a good relationship from the start and given yourself a little bit of power in a potentially powerless situation.

As time goes on, being respectful and polite to your ex's new partner can help the co-parenting relationship greatly, and helps to prevent your children from feeling guilty about spending time with them.

FINDING POWER THROUGH ACKNOWLEDGEMENT

To regain your sense of power you can:

- Contain how you feel by noticing and naming how the situation makes you feel and why.

- Acknowledge what you cannot control/impact, and focus on what you can do something about – this may be practical or emotional/psychological.
- Practise self-care and kindness toward yourself so you can regulate your emotions, process your feelings and create an overall sense of wellbeing.
- Aim to communicate in calm and fair ways, so as not to be drawn into any negativity, tit-for-tat power games or anything else that will pull you down.
- Know that you will *always* be a loving parent providing support for your child, and no matter how tough the situation is you will *always* have that important, powerful role.
- Take meaningful action where you can, in line with your values and in accordance with the parent you want to be, no matter the power dynamics at play.

So, with these principles in mind, when you feel in a situation of powerlessness, take a deep breath, and gently acknowledge, "I feel powerless right now and that makes me feel *angry/sad/ frustrated/cross/hopeless."

Follow this acknowledgement by identifying – perhaps by journaling – what *exactly* is making you feel powerless.

- What is the situation you find yourself in?
- Why does this situation bother you?
- What is happening/has happened that is making you feel powerless?
- What would you want to happen if you didn't feel powerless?
- What other perspectives are there in this situation? For example, your child's, ex-partner's or other people's?

Once you have acknowledged and understood what is out of your control and power, remind yourself that, while this is tough, it may not necessarily be a *negative* situation. For example, just because your ex-partner has control for the day, this does not mean he will do a bad job, or that the children will have a bad time. Equally, you may be powerless to prevent being a single parent right now, but this does not mean you cannot find great meaning and joy in this role in time.

Focus on what you can control and where you can find your power. This may be hard, but often there is *something* we can find, even if we find power in choosing; for example, choosing to let our anger go so it cannot have power over us. Some self-talk suggestions of finding your power include:

- "I can acknowledge I cannot magically fix everything or take away my child's, or my own, pain, and this is hard; but I can focus on finding ways to support them, and myself, through challenging situations."
- "I have power over how I look after myself and practise self-care."
- "I can seek therapy to help myself through difficult times when I feel powerless."
- "I can give my children the space to talk and process their emotions when they need to."
- "I can choose to focus on what I can control rather than the things that leave me feeling powerless. I can say to myself 'There is nothing I can do about X, this is out of my control, take a deep breath and let that part go. In the meantime, I can focus on Y.'"
- "I can live by values that are important to me, such as kindness, forgiveness, respect, patience, cooperation."
- "I can be assertive in how I communicate and act in situations with my ex-partner."

FINDING POWER THROUGH MANAGING EMOTIONS

When emotions become overwhelming they can have power over us. Helping to contain and regulate our own emotions or those of our children can help in regaining a sense of power.

Making Sense of Your Own Emotions

In any given situation this can mean taking the following steps:

- Name the emotion you are feeling.
- Notice where you feel this in your body.
- Imagine turning toward your emotions rather than away from them. Do not try to push them away (this is rarely successful).
- Take a deep breath and breathe into your emotions. Make space for where you feel this in your body.
- Acknowledge you feel this way, and this is tough. Practise sitting with the emotion and asking yourself what you need right now. And then do what you need (self-care).
- If a situation makes you sad, angry, guilty, etc, look at the relevant chapters for ideas of how to manage these emotions.

Following these steps means you are compassionately listening to your emotions, acknowledging them, making space for them and responding to what you need in that moment with care.

Making Sense of Your Children's Emotions

Helping your child make sense of their own emotions is important too. As parents we are not able to shield our children from difficult experiences or emotions, but we *can* provide a safe and supportive space for our child/children to process their emotions – and that is an incredibly powerful gift for life that we can give them, teaching them lifelong skills in the process. We can do this by:

- Listening, and letting them talk or express their feelings.
- Where appropriate, comforting them through physical presence or touch (holding hands, hugs or just being there, close by).
- Comforting them with words, validating how they feel and letting them know you are there for comfort. This shows you have listened and have heard how they feel. You can say something like, "I can hear you really miss Daddy. I know it is hard. It is okay to miss him. How do you feel/what is it like for you?", or "It sounds like it is making you feel sad. I understand it's really tough. It is sad. I'm here anytime you want to talk about this. Shall we have a hug?".
- Don't dismiss them or convince them it's all okay or that they shouldn't feel sad. Although it can be painful to hear, let them express their feelings and know that is okay.

From Powerless to Powerful: Finding your Power

1. Self-talk can be very empowering. Stand or sit in front of a mirror, and say to yourself:
   - "I can find my way as a single mother."
   - "It may not be my choice to be here, but I can be courageous and find meaning and joy in this journey nonetheless."
   - "This is my journey, and I get to choose how it will be."
   - "I am free to choose how I want my home, my routines, my life to be."
   - "There will be situations I cannot control, and I can learn to live with this, as there will always be something in my power that I can focus on."
   - "I can bring myself peace and happiness by letting go of the things I cannot control and by focusing on what I can do and how I can live."
2. Look at all the areas of your life and acknowledge where you have your power. Focus on these – it could be how you decorate your house, when you go to bed, what you choose to cook, the music you listen to, how you choose to parent your children, and so on.
3. Remind yourself, "I have power in my life in many small (and big) ways. I may not have power in *every* way, but where I do is where I can find power as a single mum."

8

FINDING JOY

If your break-up is still very raw, although you might not feel it right now, we promise that you will feel joy once more. The aim of this chapter is to help you find joy in the everyday and hold on to happiness even during the darkest moments.

While big wins, such as securing a car or purchasing a flat, are clearly cause for celebration, joy also comes from seemingly little things – a bike ride through the countryside, a dinnertime without battles, cuddles with the kids on the sofa, a child-free night with a soldier (ahem) …

> *My first glimmer of joy occurred when something that seemed like an unfathomable dream happened. That's right – I fixed my broken boiler on my own. That moment, when I realized that I don't need a man in my life to deal with tricky things, will be forever etched in my brain.* **Amy**

WHAT IS JOY?

Joy can be described as a feeling of pleasure, delight, great happiness. Dr Pamela King, a developmental psychologist and researcher, has focused her work on understanding joy. She explains that:

> "... many people have an enduring and underlying sense of something that is deeper than the emotion of happiness, and I have come to describe this as joy ... joy is more complex than a feeling or an emotion. It is something one can practice, cultivate, or make a habit ... joy is an enduring, deep delight in what holds the most significance ... we can discover and experience joy in a variety of ways – doing those things we love to do, growing in intimacy or providing for others, and clarifying and coherently pursuing our values."
>
> (Psychology Today interview, What is Joy and What Does it Say About Us? 2020)

This is a wonderful description and helps to guide us to think about ways we can cultivate, and actively encourage joy to be present in our lives. As a single mother, you absolutely deserve this!

FEELING JOY (OR NOT)

Joy, happiness, fun, delight, excitement, pleasure, contentment, satisfaction, cheerfulness, amusement, laughter, relaxation. How do you feel when you read these words? Do they make you want to smile, remind you of a time you have experienced these feelings, or make you feel sad that you are struggling to feel these emotions right now?

Whichever it is for you, know that it is okay to feel like that, because the human experience is made up of a range of emotions. Sadness, anger, worry, happiness, guilt, irritation, joy, excitement, stress, and many more. As humans, it is normal to feel all these emotions at some point, and we often move through these different emotions during our day or our week. Knowing this is important in understanding that the presence of heavier emotions – sadness, grief, anger – does not mean we cannot also find moments of happiness, fun, joy, excitement.

ACT pioneer Dr Russ Harris has talked about the concept of the "Happiness Trap", which is the idea that it is an unachievable aim to think we should be happy all the time. It is not how we are set up as humans to only have happiness. But we can strive to experience *times* of happiness, to recognize and allow it in when it shows up, to find it in our lives by taking active steps to do things that make us laugh and bring us joy. This we *can* do and this we *can* achieve – no matter what other emotions or challenging situations may be present.

On the journey into single motherhood, we may of course experience *all* the heavy situations and emotions: grief, anger, rage, shame, anxiety, depression, and more. We have to make space for these emotions, allow ourselves to acknowledge them and process them. Yet in the depths of these, we can also allow ourselves to find the lighter emotions, and know that, as time goes on and by taking helpful steps forward, we can also find the light more and more. And with this we can find our fun, our happiness, our laughter, our joy, our sunshine. Know this, give yourself permission for this, feel this, believe in this.

HOW DO WE FIND JOY?

Finding our sunshine, our joy, is not always a simple task. Sometimes we may have to work really hard to find it, and sometimes it may find us easily.

Allowing yourself to be open to joy, happiness, laughter if it arises is a good place to start. Knowing it is okay to laugh even in your grief, knowing it is okay to be silly and play even within depression, knowing it is okay to feel excited and amused, even when we feel angry, is a first step. And over time you will find more and more of this in your life, and it will feel easier and easier to find it and feel it.

It is also important to notice how you speak to yourself, and to gently draw your narrative toward happiness and joy. This isn't about effectively gaslighting yourself by forcing only a positive narrative and ignoring how you are really thinking and feeling – that is not helpful; it is about trying any combination of the following:

- Speak to yourself honestly and compassionately – life may be hard right now, *and* you can also be open to finding joy despite the darkness.
- Remind yourself you deserve joy and happiness, no matter what your path has been to single motherhood.
- Keep an eye on the self-critical voice inside who may constantly criticise you, your choices, your behaviours – a stream of self-criticism doesn't help anyone.
- Remind yourself there are no prizes for working yourself into the ground by only focusing on work, chores, parenting tasks and so on. Allowing yourself time for fun and enjoyment, for seeking joy, will help you, and will help your children by allowing you to be a happier, more relaxed parent. You will also be modelling for your child the importance of fun and enjoyment and time off in life.
- Allow your mind to focus on gratitude. Gratitude practices allow you to find moments of gratitude even in hard times. Again, this isn't about ignoring the challenges of a situation, but about finding moments of gratitude within them. This helps us develop new narratives in our mind that notice the good, the positive, the light, which can help us be more open to joy and happiness when it comes our way.

"The more you praise and celebrate your life, the more there is in life to celebrate."

Oprah Winfrey, TV personality, actress, author and philanthropist

Gratitude Practices

1. Think about three things that you are grateful for in your life right now, for example:
   - Yourself – your strength, your resilience, your love and care
   - Your children
   - Another person who brings something good to your life
   - Your health or the health of loved ones
   - Your ability to move, dance, play
   - The weather – the sunshine, even the rain
   - Your pets
   - Your home – having a roof over your head, heating, food, nice things
   - Your freedom
2. With each gratitude you identify, take a moment to close your eyes, really think and feel your gratitude for what you have identified. Feel it in your body. Think about how this really makes a difference in a meaningful way in your life.
3. Talk with your children, or let yourself think, about how grateful, thankful, lucky you are to have these areas of gratitude in your life.
4. Keep a gratitude journal, and write down something you are grateful for every day.

"Gratitude is the wine for the soul. Go on. Get drunk."
Rumi, poet

Take some time to think about what does bring you joy – what do you love, what makes you laugh, what inspires you, excites you, amuses you, brings you happiness? This may be about finding new things just for you, or for you and your child together. It may take time to try new things and discover what works for you.

TWENTY PRINCIPLES FOR FINDING JOY

There are some active steps we can take to find moments of joy and happiness. Finding what brings you joy in everyday life is so important, but acknowledging it and appreciating it is even more so. People that can realize their joys (no matter how big or small) tend to live a happier, less stressed life. Exactly what we want, right? Go and find this in your life, because you deserve it.

1. Breathe and be in the present. Learn about mindfulness – being caught in the past or the future by our minds can make it difficult to just enjoy where we are.
2. Play with your kids – hell, even act like a kid! The joy it brings to their faces is contagious.
3. Be *you* – wear what you love, colour your hair however you want.
4. Date yourself – do nice things for *you* – pamper yourself, take yourself out for dinner, buy yourself gifts or flowers.
5. Make meaningful connections with friends, neighbours, family, colleagues.

6. Surround yourself with people that help you to feel good – quality is more important than quantity when it comes to friends.

7. Celebrate *you* – both small wins and big wins.

8. Get outside – see sunsets, forests, the sea, beautiful gardens, wild flowers, city landscapes. Pause and notice these. Find the beauty around you.

9. Let things go – worry, anger, guilt, resentment, jealousy, shame. Let yourself know you have the power to let these go, be compassionate to yourself, forgive yourself.

10. Find joy and gratitude in small things, small moments.

11. Find your fitness through an activity that you love.

12. Listen to music that lifts your mood, energizes you, inspires you, empowers you.

13. Practise kindness and compassion for yourself and others – tell a stranger you like their outfit/hair/nails; get dressed up and take an amazing selfie and admire yourself.

14. Do something you are proud of – volunteer, challenge yourself, tackle a new skill, a random act of kindness.

15. Watch, listen to or read things that make you laugh.

16. Get creative and learn to do something that you love – cook, write, paddleboard, yoga, paint.

17. Go out there and find your happiness and joy, don't wait for it to come to you – work for it, plan for it.

18. Keep a note of what makes you happy, what is good in your life, what you enjoy, what makes you laugh.

19. Make a list of your future plans, what you want to achieve, would like to try, what you will love to do in the future – your own joyful bucket list.

20. Be open to love – both loving others and being loved – and laugh and smile every single day.

STORIES OF JOY IN SINGLE MOTHERHOOD

Joy can be found in something as simple as sending messages between yourself and your friends.

> **Ellie** *loves the interactions she has online.*
> *"I really appreciate when friends reach out to me or send me funny memes now more than ever."*

Realize that you have the power to change things in your new life as a single parent, which can help bring you joy.

> **Frenchie** *started a new job as a single mum.*
> *"I started working in a care home last year, which is something I never would have had the courage to do as my past self, and I love it. I can feel the richness building within me and this new version of myself being moulded, and I absolutely love her."*

> **Emilia** *shared:*
> *"For me the joy has come from having no one to answer to in terms of the life choices I've made. Be it home décor or choosing to leave the dishes in the sink until the morning, I have freedom and feel like I'm not being judged."*

Think about your daily routine, and how you might initiate joyful moments throughout your routine or how you might turn situations that have been frustrating to deal with into pleasant situations. Perhaps setting the alarm a little earlier would give you some extra time to savour your morning coffee before the rush of the day kicks in? Maybe organizing a fun park trip after school will help you to spend some time with other people and burn your child's energy off a little. Maybe set a new tradition of a kitchen disco while you make dinner – get the kids to join in and buy a disco light – have fun, be silly, find joy!

Ellie *changed up the bedtime routine to better suit her.*

"It usually takes a while for my little girl to fall asleep, so I've started making a cup of tea and taking that up with me and sitting beside her and just savouring that time. Instead of stressing about it, I try and see it as relaxation time for me and a chance to have a cuddle with her; a lot of the time it's the best part of my day."

While all the little joyful moments are absolutely necessary, isn't it an amazing feeling to have a big win? It's so easy for life to get in the way and for us to ignore all the wonderful things we do, and whether it's getting a new job, finishing a project or running a marathon, you deserve to pop open the bubbly and celebrate your amazing achievements.

When **Ellie** *was married, she sold her car because they didn't need two. Soon after, her daughter's dad left.*

"For a good year and a half, I didn't have my own car, but recently I was able to sort out a car for myself. It's made me feel so happy, and like I've got some freedom back."

Kelly *managed to buy out her ex-partner and secure their flat for herself and her son.*

"It was so hard to do – financially, emotionally, legally – and I was so proud of myself."

Whether it's your child telling you they love you, or chats before bedtime, those kids of ours sure know how to lift the spirits (and bring them down – this parenting malarkey is an emotional rollercoaster).

I collected my son from school the other day and he had made me a card – for no reason. It had a picture of us holding hands among flowers and said, "To mummy, I love you, love from milo xxx". I cried, and framed it. Now I look at that whenever I'm feeling crappy, and it reminds me that I am actually alright. If my kid decides to make me a card just to tell me he loves me, rather than drawing another Minecraft picture, then I can't be doing a too shabby job of single parenting. **Amy**

Arabella *had a moment with some schoolwork.*

"The teacher asked me to speak to her and handed me my son's RE book. He had written a poem about me and was given a headteacher's award for his beautiful handwriting. I cried! It made me realize that I can do this – I am a single mum, and my child is happy."

If you feel like you don't have enough time with your child (or if the time you do have is fraught, busy and the opposite of "quality"), it's worth considering whether there may be something you can change in your weekly routine to plan some fun things where you can find the joy together.

I choose to take mine swimming every Wednesday, no matter how busy I am with work. It's our time to be together, without screens and distractions – just fun in the pool! **Amy**

Katie *found joy through small things.*

"I prioritized special weekly movie nights with the kids, where we made popcorn and got treats like in the cinema, and then we also went and did things that the kids loved but right out of the comfort zone – once we went to an

inflatable water park. It was So. Much. Fun. Despite the cold lake and the wetsuits, it absolutely made us laugh so much and really felt like joy."

HOW SOME AMAZING SINGLE MUMS FIND JOY

- "Blasting a playlist into the bathroom cheers me up every morning during my five minutes of peace while getting ready."
- "Learning paddleboarding yoga!"
- "Listening to a podcast that makes me laugh so much I nearly wet myself." (Rob Beckett and Josh Widdicombe's *Parenting Hell*)
- "Learning to bake."
- "Buying some really nice night moisturizer."
- "Buying myself flowers once a week."
- "Getting a kitten."
- "Doing an inflatable water course."
- "Learning to play Mario Kart with my son."
- "Going for a morning walk by the river when I don't have the children."
- "Learning a new hobby – restoring old furniture."
- "Once my children were old enough I developed a new routine of having a cup of tea in bed every Saturday morning, while they had some screen time. I bought a lovely breakfast tray, would open the curtains, get my book and have some moments of peace and it felt so good."
- "Putting my phone away and building Lego with my son."

- "When my youngest goes to bed and my elder daughter and I are watching a film together."
- "Binge-watching trashy TV."
- "Having a big bubble bath, bath tray, glass of wine, music, candles – heaven!"
- "Getting a facial – my skin has never felt so good!"
- "Going to the pub for a pint on my child-free nights!"
- "Teaching my daughter to ride her bike."

HOW TO HOLD ON TO THE HAPPINESS AND FIND JOY DURING THE DARK TIMES

We all know single parenting can be really heavy and challenging at times, and there will be plenty of times where you struggle to find joy. So how can we hold on to the happiness and joy during the dark times?

- Actively seek out the good, the happy, the joy. If it's been a rubbish day, think about what you can do to bring you some good.
- Remind yourself joy can be found even in the darkest times.
- Practise a joyful compassionate self-talk exercise (see below).
- Create a Finding Joy jar – write down all your ideas for what brings you joy and pleasure or what you would like to do. Your children can join in too. Pick ones you can try and plan these in.
- Create a journal of your joyful successes. Every time you feel happy, write down what has brought you joy. When you're struggling to see the joy in life, read all those happy memories you have.

- Get outside. Spending time outside, even if it's just for a short walk, can do you the world of good. You might not feel like it, but try anyway.
- Create a joyful playlist (or a playlist for when you need to feel the rage, that is okay too!) – music can be inspiring.

Joyful Self-talk Exercise

1. Close your eyes, reach up high, and stretch your arms out wide (like you have just won a race).
2. Smile and say to yourself:
   - "I deserve joy."
   - "I can find happiness."
   - "I can bring fun into my life."
3. Allow yourself to know this, feel this.
4. Now, if you like, do this again. How does that feel?

Combine this with the Kind Hands exercise on page 83.
1. Place a hand on your heart, feel the warmth radiating inward, and close your eyes.
2. Smile to yourself and repeat the phrases above.

OUR JOYFUL PLAYLIST

Studies have shown how music can change our mood, particularly helping to lift our mood. Music can make you feel empowered, strong, hopeful, happy. Music can help you experience, feel and process your emotions – the right song can help you express your anger, feel your sadness, acknowledge your loneliness; and the right song can also make you want to sing, dance, smile, laugh.

Would any of the tracks below make it on to your playlist? Feel free to choose from this list or create your own – just promise to dance round the kitchen and find your joy!

- "Hold On" – Wilson Phillips
- "Reach" – S Club 7
- "R.E.S.P.E.C.T." – Aretha Franklin
- "Don't Stop Me Now" – Queen
- "Happy" – Pharrell Williams
- "Walking on Sunshine" – Katrina and the Waves
- "Brave" – Sara Bareilles
- "Get Back Up Again" – Anna Kendrick
- "Good as Hell" – Lizzo
- "Can't Stop the Feeling!" – Justin Timberlake
- "One Day Like This" – Elbow
- "Run the World (Girls)" – Beyoncé
- "On Top of the World" – Imagine Dragons
- "Live your Life" – Nick Cordero
- "Survivor" – Destiny's Child
- "Roar" – Katy Perry
- "Fight Song" – Rachel Platten
- "No Scrubs" – TLC
- "Love my Life" – Robbie Williams
- "Dreams" – Fleetwood Mac
- "I Got The Juice" – Janelle Monáe
- "We Are Young" – fun.
- "Monster" – Dodie

Your task: Find some time this week to make yourself a joy playlist – include anything that inspires you, uplifts you, makes you smile, dance, move, sing.

FINDING JOY

Our final note on joy: No matter how tough things feel right now, believe in finding joy, believe that you deserve joy. Gently, slowly, you can find ways to let the light in.

9

LOVE, LUST AND EVERYTHING IN BETWEEN

There will come a time where you feel ready to start dating again, be it in a few months or years. The prospect might sound super exciting or incredibly daunting, both feelings that are completely valid when it comes to opening up your heart (or legs) to a potential suitor!

Whether you're looking for some casual fun or are ready to find your very own Ryan Reynolds, it can help to know what you are looking for before entering the big world of dating – do you want to go on a few dates with someone, or are you simply looking for a notch on your bedpost? Also, how much time do you have? Do you really want to be spending your one night a week off on a rubbish date? So much to consider!

SORRY, BUT SELF-LOVE COMES FIRST

As you heal from your relationship breakdown, being around happy couples may throw an array of emotions at you. It can be an emotional rollercoaster; being around happy couples might make you feel jealous, sad, hopeful, angry, or even anxious.

It sucks. It totally sucks. Thoughts like "Why can't I be happy?", "Why do they get to be happy and I'm not?", "Will I ever be loved again?", "What's wrong with me?" and "How can I cope without a partner?" can encompass you. You don't want these negative thoughts when you're around stable, happy relationships, but you can't help it.

You should not feel bad about having these feelings, this is all part of your healing process, and you will indeed heal. Just take your time. But in the words of the oh-so-wise Ru Paul, "If you don't love yourself, how in the hell you gonna love somebody else?"

HOW TO LEARN TO LOVE YOURSELF

- Kill comparison. Don't compare yourself to others, you are your own, unique you – and you are beyond comparable.
- Appreciate your strengths and qualities. Learn to love the best bits of you – get to know yourself and who you are and what you stand for.
- Practise self-acceptance. Rather than striving for perfection, practise telling yourself you are good just as you are, and mean it, for all your strengths and your (perceived) flaws. It doesn't mean you can't choose self-improvement, but you can do that with compassion for yourself and accept yourself right now.
- Take the pressure off. Banish "I should …" self-talk – where you are right now is okay. This doesn't mean you can't begin to work on goals and aims for the future, but change "I should …" into "I'd like to …".
- Plan for the future. Make a bucket list for your new life, your new future, whether that be learning to bake, taking up horse riding, travelling, getting a tattoo – or all of those things and more.
- Treat yourself. You deserve more of what makes you happy, whether it's a slice of cake with your tea or those shoes you've been lusting after.

- Forgive yourself. We all make mistakes, if we beat ourselves up about them forever we're never going to have a good relationship with ourselves.
- Accept the haters. Some people won't like you, that's a given. But do you need everyone to like you? That's a hell of a lot of pressure.
- Have fun. Try to schedule at least one fun thing in each week – something you love to do, something that brings you joy.
- Celebrate success. Write down the things you have nailed – even if it was something as simple as finishing reading a book or cleaning the bathroom!
- Try a hobby. When was the last time you did something for you? Think about all the things you've thought about trying, now go and try one!
- Exercise. Exercise releases endorphins, and endorphins make us happy! Try to squeeze in a little bit of exercise each day – even if it's something like walking to the store instead of driving.
- Ask for help! When you need some extra support, go get it – the weight of the world doesn't need to be on your shoulders alone.
- Set boundaries. If you want to say no to an event, you can bloody well say no. You need to do what is good for you, so don't let anyone pressure you into doing things you don't want to.

Appreciating You

1. Get some paper or a journal, or even your phone or laptop.

2. Write down all the strengths, qualities, skills, values that you bring to friendships, work, parenting, relationships. As you do this, be sure to notice and shush that critical voice – we don't need to give that attention right now. This is about engaging your kind compassionate voice, the one you use for your friends and loved ones.

3. Use "I" statements: "I'm kind", "I'm thoughtful", "I'm hard working", "I'm funny", "I'm doing my best", "I'm a good listener", "I'm adventurous" …

4. Once you've finished writing, see if you can decorate a whole page with your words – try using different writing styles and sizes (or fonts and type sizes), art, doodles, stickers, emojis, cut-out images from magazines.

5. And, just for a moment, celebrate YOU. You deserve it.

STORIES OF LOVE AND LUST IN SINGLE MOTHERHOOD

LEARNING YOU DON'T NEED A RELATIONSHIP, BUT IT'S OKAY TO WANT ONE

You may be someone who has gone through life more often in a relationship than out of one, or you may be someone who is naturally okay not being in a relationship. Whichever it is, it can help to understand your patterns and what being in a relationship means to you. How do you feel when you are in a relationship and when you are out of one?

If you have always felt defined by a relationship, and feel fully lost outside of one, it can be tempting to want to rush straight into another one. And this may be how you have always rolled – before kids. However, once you have children in the mix, this can make this dating strategy more difficult; finding a new companion is harder to put into place once you're a single parent, and it is important to be really kind to yourself about this. It can help to take some time, and possibly some therapy if helpful, to understand who you are *outside* of a relationship and why relationships are so important to you, and to help yourself be okay just as you are, not defined by or completed by a relationship, but just you.

It can be healthy for you to take some time to look after you and to learn to love yourself. Let yourself know that a relationship can absolutely come in time, once you've had a chance to focus on yourself.

Roxy shared:

"After my marriage ended through infidelity, I was overwhelmed; but then I threw myself into wanting to be loved again far too quicky. I just really wanted to feel loved and special and unique to someone. Looking back, I don't have any regrets for all that early dating as there is no point, it was all part of my healing process. I did find dating utterly terrifying and fascinating at the same time. I had so many adventures, and I have to say I enjoyed the journey, but I wasn't really ready to find that special person – also, it can take a while to find them! Dating didn't fill that void that I had inside; I realized that needed to come from working on me."

For others, it can be an active choice to not be in a relationship, and instead focus on being a single mum.

Ishana *actively made the choice to stay single during the early years.*

"I had some struggles at the beginning with my daughter's dad being on and off the scene. Once I knew he really wasn't going to stick around, I was going through so much I just wanted to focus on me and my girl. This was a choice I was happy to make. I wanted to enjoy the time we had together, and we had such fun building our new life with friends and family, I just didn't need anyone else in the mix. I always knew I would explore dating again at some point, but I just didn't need to at that time, and haven't for 10 years. I'm really happy with my choice."

KNOWING WHEN YOU'RE READY

Opening yourself up to romance can be a great confidence booster (if it goes well!). However, there is the potential of causing yourself more hurt if you jump in before you're ready. It's all in the timing.

For example, if you're still completely hung up on your ex, getting out into the world of dating is probably not for you. While you might feel like you want that companionship of a partner again, there is no rush to start dating. Even if your ex has already moved on, you don't have to do the same to show to the world that you're okay.

Try not to rush into dating out of fear of being alone or being single for the rest of your life. Some women fear that time is ticking, and they have to meet someone before it is too late; this can especially be the case if you want to get married or want more children and feel you are on a countdown to be able to achieve these things. However, rushing into a relationship when you aren't ready will never be worth it.

Around two weeks after my son's father left, I was tempted by the world of online dating – my friends were using Tinder and I had never experienced it before. So, I uploaded the most flattering pictures I could find and started swiping. Pretty quickly, the matches began flowing in and I was on cloud nine knowing that there were men out there who found me attractive. All good, right? Wrong. It had been two weeks since I had experienced the worst heartache I've ever known, so this was bound to affect my mental health. I started getting to know a man. We were messaging almost constantly for a few days, and then I had an anxiety attack. I convinced myself that he was, in fact, a murderer and I shouldn't have been so foolish to start talking to a stranger from the internet – it goes against everything we were taught while growing up! In hindsight, I realize I was simply not ready to be having these experiences yet. **Amy**

Jemma's initial experience of dating showed her she wasn't ready yet.

"I wasn't even interested in or thinking about dating for two years after my relationship ended. Friends would suggest this to me, but at that time it was so simple to say no. I had no interest whatsoever, even though my ex-partner had moved on after a year of our separation. In this time, a friend separated from her husband, and began dating again after a month of him moving out. And it worked out really well for her, so she encouraged me to try it, but I just knew it wasn't for me yet. After about two and a half years, I began to consider dating, and the only option really seemed to be via online. I didn't know any single people, and didn't meet people through work. I began trying some of the online apps, and although I did find it fun, and it was a boost to get likes and chat with people, I also found the heartache of rejection, people not swiping or messaging back (even though I knew I was doing the same to other people) was just too much, too upsetting. I still wasn't quite ready."

Katie was terrified of dating when she first began exploring three years after her divorce.

"People would tell me how fun it was to go out and date different people, and I just couldn't see it. For a long time I couldn't even imagine it. Slowly this changed. I'm a pretty shy person, and the idea of meeting new people and them not liking me was excruciating. But I got used to chatting online and began to get a sense of people I liked and could easily chat to and ones I just didn't get on with. Eventually, I began meeting people. I could share so many stories! There was the one who was brilliant at chatting and then just disappeared online one day. I still don't know why, and I will admit that hurt. But it taught me to be a little wary and to be careful to know who you are chatting to online, which wasn't a bad thing to learn. Then there was the one who lied about his height and hid behind a pillar to put hairspray on before he met me; and he tried to send me semi-naked pictures after I'd told him I wasn't interested. I was able to laugh at this, but it was actually NOT OKAY. Then there were the lovely ones – ones I've stayed friends with, ones who were kind, ones who were really funny. I am so much more confident now in dating and I do know it is fun, when you are ready."

TAKE YOUR TIME

It can feel especially hard as a woman if you feel your biological clock is working against you. However, trying to rush something you aren't ready for is unlikely to ever end up going well. If you aren't emotionally in a good enough place to love yourself or to have processed the loss and hurt you have just been through, or to find your place securely as a single mother, then you won't be in a healthy place to develop a healthy relationship.

Take your time to process everything you have been through, and to find stability in your new life. This will put you in a much better place to find a date and, ultimately, a relationship that is going to work for you. Taking the time to do this will be worth it, and will hopefully save you from unhealthy relationships. You often have much more time than you think.

QUIZ: ARE YOU READY TO DATE AGAIN?

Take this fun quiz to assess whether you're ready for the dating game or not. Circle one of "a", "b" and "c" for each question.

1. **How much do you love yourself?**

   a) I feel worthless
   b) I quite like myself
   c) I am a goddess

2. **When did you last stalk your ex's social media?**

   a) A few hours ago
   b) Within the last week
   c) Can't even remember, mate!

3. **If your ex asked for you back, what would you say?**

   a) Take me, take me now!
   b) Hmm, I don't know …
   c) HELL NO, GET AWAY FROM ME!

4. **The thought of going on a date with someone makes you feel:**

   a) Sad
   b) Intrigued
   c) Excited

5. **Why do you want to start dating?**

   a) To fill a void in my life
   b) Because I'm bored
   c) To meet new people and have fun new experiences

6. **What do you want from a date?**

   a) To meet the love of my life
   b) To boost my confidence
   c) An orgasm

7. **How do you feel about being single?**

   a) I hate it, I need an "other half"
   b) It's a bit lonely at times
   c) I'm fine with it

8. **Do you have the energy to date?**

   a) Nah, I'm tired just thinking about it
   b) I guess I could muster up some energy for it
   c) Yes. Come at me!

9. **Do you feel hopeful about the future when it comes to finding someone new?**

   a) Never gonna happen
   b) I'm trying to be
   c) Yes, for sure!

10. **Are your friends/family encouraging you to date?**

    a) No, they don't think I'm ready
    b) We don't talk about it
    c) Yes, they're really supportive

Give yourself three points for every "a", two points for every "b" and one point for every "c" answer. Total up your points.

22 to 30 points

Hey, you! You need to focus on *yourself* and find a way to love YOU before you give your attention to other humans.

17 to 21 points

Maybe dip your toes into the dating game and see how you feel. A night of fun might be just what the doctor ordered. Just don't go moving them into your house next week, okay?

10 to 16 points

Go on out there and get some! You're ready for all the fun, just stay safe!

KNOW WHAT YOU ARE LOOKING FOR

Whether you're new to dating, having only ever been with one person before or you have a lot of experience of dating, it is important to take some time to think about what you are looking for right now, as a single parent. Do you want something casual or are you looking for long-term potential? Do you want to explore the sexual part of dating, or companionship to walk and chat/text, or to be wined and dined? You might be ready to meet lots of different people and be really open to whatever matches you find, or you might have a very specific idea in mind of what you want. Whatever you want is okay, but it is important to take some time to find out exactly what you want, and don't be afraid to stick to your guns to find it.

ONLINE DATING

Long gone are the days of casually bumping into someone in a club, exchanging numbers and awaiting true love. While it would be great to meet someone naturally through work or friends, or at a bar, in reality online dating is generally the way to go these days.

There are lots of dating apps available, whatever your sexual preference. Most of them share similar features: you create a profile with a picture and some information about you, you set some filters to narrow your options, and off you go. Many have the system of swiping left or right, depending on if you are interested or not, and most will show you people in your local area. Some of the most popular apps include:

- Tinder – while many on this app are interested in casual relationships and one-night stands, there are people looking for longer-term relationships too; just don't be surprised if you get some fairly sexual approaches!

- Bumble – this app is directed at giving the women more of the say, as the man can only chat with you once you have made the first move. There is a mix of people looking for one-night stands and relationships. You can also use the app just to find friends.

- Hinge – this app is a mix of elements of Tinder and Bumble, but, unlike Bumble, anyone can make the first approach.

- Match – this app tends to attract those looking for something longer term, and the approach is less sexual than you might find on other apps.

- Eharmony – this app is very similar to Match, with participants often looking for relationships.

- Her – this app is a great option for queer, nonbinary, trans and gender-nonconforming people. As well as having a dating aspect, it also includes a calendar of events and a forum.

CREATING A PROFILE

The world of online dating does pose a whole load of new questions and worries, such as: how much information should you share with complete strangers?

You'll want to think about choosing a few favourite pictures – recent ones will help you in the long term if you don't want your date to be shocked when you don't match your youthful photo from ten years ago!

Think about how much you want someone else to know about you. For example, stating your relationship status (for example, divorced) and how many children you have helps rule out people who won't be interested in a divorced mum. But it is your personal choice whether you want potential dates to know these details right away.

Be careful about how much you share on your public profile. We wouldn't recommend sharing pictures of your children – remember, this profile could be seen by thousands of people and you can't control that information once it is out there. Nor do we recommend sharing too much identifiable personal information on your profile; until you are sure who you are talking to and that you trust them with your information it is best to be a little wary.

THE PROCESS

Create a profile, swipe for people you like, chat with them, and – if this all works – you might swap numbers. An initial video call is a good idea to see how they actually look, sound and act – and, if you like what you see, plan a date.

Take care to follow all the dating app guidance on meeting people safely. If you go on a date, make sure you let a friend know where you are and who you are meeting. Meet in a public place and (hopefully) enjoy! It can also be good to plan how you will leave if you aren't enjoying the date or you know it isn't a match for you. Don't feel you have to end up in a goodbye kiss if they aren't for you! Saying no can, of course, be excruciating, but you must practise this for you and your date's benefit.

PITFALLS

Please be aware of all of the following:

- Catfishing. This is where the person isn't who they claim to be in their online profile; they may have stolen someone else's pictures or identity. Always follow the site's online safety advice, and if a person is completely avoiding showing you their actual self then you would be right to be suspicious. Unfortunately, there are people online who will take advantage, given the opportunity.

- Explicit material. You may experience receiving unwanted messages or photos, which can feel shocking and violating. This isn't okay. Please do not tolerate anything you are uncomfortable with and, of course, be very careful sharing anything explicit yourself. There is nothing wrong with this communication between two consenting adults, but it is wise to be careful of what you share as once photos or messages are out there you may have no control what happens to them. Dating apps allow you to "unmatch" without any explanation, which can help reduce unwanted messages; you can also report inappropriate profiles to the dating sites.

DATING AND CHILDREN

You might be ready to start dating, but may be wondering how this works now you are a single mum. We will talk a bit more in the next chapter about introducing your children to your new relationship, but in the early days of dating here are some things you may want to consider.

- You don't have as much free time as you did pre-children, so it will take more planning and organizing to find time for you to date.
- If your date isn't prepared to be flexible with your availability then they aren't for you, as this is the reality of your life and there will be plenty out there who will be able to work with you on this.
- It is okay to prioritize your children.
- It is okay to not involve your children, or even talk about your children, if you don't want to, in early dating. In these early days you can focus on you and your date, and once

the relationship builds you may share more as you feel comfortable.

Depending on the ages of your children, your dating life may be very separate to your children and parenting life, and that is okay; for young children especially, it would be a lot for them to process until you are sure it is a relationship that will last. Some teenage children will be keen to know, others will not – respect where they are in their emotional journey. None of this means keeping secrets – open honesty is always best – but be mindful that the speed with which your children process the separation/family changes may be different to yours, and even if you are ready to date, they may not be ready for this.

"WOULD YOU DATE A SINGLE MUM?"

Amy actually went online, swiped right for a bucketload of potential suitors, and posed the question: "What is your honest opinion on dating a single mum?" While there were a mixed bag of responses, the main concerns from those questioned appeared to be how they would make a relationship work around the child and how involved the mum would expect them to be.

Dating someone with a child isn't for everyone, and if you can tell your match about your family situation sooner rather than later, you're less likely to waste your time and feelings on someone that isn't right for you and your little family.

HOW TO DATE AND ENJOY IT!

The dating experience can be terrifying, but it can also be so much fun. Dating can give you the opportunity to be you – to be you as a single woman, not you the parent, not you the school mum, not you the work colleague. You get to have some time for you.

It can help to look at dating as an opportunity to meet new people, to talk to another adult just about yourselves, to share stories, to try something new. You can be who you want to be and there is something very freeing in that. And if it doesn't work for you, you just walk away. You can take it as an opportunity to dress up and pamper yourself. You get to feel the excitement of feeling attractive in yourself and know someone else is thinking this too.

Of course you may well be anxious, terrified even, of meeting someone new. What will you say, how will you act? Will they like you? It is perfectly normal to have all these thoughts and feelings and more. However, try not to let them overtake you. Find yourself a mantra to repeat, such as: "You are deserving of enjoying a date and finding someone new and nice – they will likely be just as nervous about meeting you". Whether the date works out or it turns out to be one you will laugh about later and chalk up to experience, it is always an adventure you can take with you and grow from.

Jemma found dating was escapism.
"My life was so heavy and full of work and parenting and chores. I loved meeting people who lived somewhere else to me, with different lives and jobs and so on. I could go and see them or go out for dinner, and just be away from my life for a while. For a while I just enjoyed dating, without any plan for a long-term commitment. I didn't want to talk about the children or about the heaviness of parts of my life. I just wanted to have fun, talk about the world, listen to music, watch a film, have a lovely dinner. That was enough! It was my little escape, and it was so good for me."

DATING AND BOUNDARY SETTING

Only you know what your boundaries need to be, so focus on what works for you and be sure to set those boundaries clearly. You may have boundaries about how much you share online, about pictures you share or receive, about how far things progress on a first, second, third date. You may have boundaries about how you expect to be treated, about communication and behaviour. Whatever your boundaries, it is okay to hold them, and you do not have to apologize for them.

Some basic boundaries could (and perhaps should) include:

- If you see any red flags – run for the hills! Trust your instincts on this.
- Only date people who respect you and your commitments as a single mum. If they can't show you (or your child commitments) the respect you deserve, then they need to leave.
- Stay away from the emotionally unavailable – it'll do you more harm than good.
- Think about when you'd be happy to get intimate with someone – if they try to pressure you or cross a line inappropriately or too soon, then they too have got to go. Learn to say no.

BUILDING RESILIENCE AND KEEPING YOUR CONFIDENCE

While joining the dating game can help to boost your confidence to begin with, what happens when you get talking to an amazing person on an app … you are getting on really well and then … you're ghosted. You've opened yourself up to someone and then you're hit with the harsh reality that they've not chosen you. It's a knockback, especially when it comes to confidence.

This is why developing self-love, acceptance of yourself and confidence in who you are is so important before you jump back into the dating saddle. Regularly practising things to help you love yourself will help you deal with these confidence knocks. Ultimately, you need to be okay as you are and be dating because you want to, not as a way to seek validation from someone else.

REJECTION AND RESILIENCE

The dating experience can be brutal for having to face and cope with "rejection" fairly regularly (if you are swiping on dating apps). For every person you may match with there may be another who doesn't match, or un-matches, or doesn't reply to your messages. This is the reality of today's dating experience and you have to build up a big wedge of resilience to cope with this.

We say "rejection" in inverted commas, because it is important that we highlight that this is not a true rejection of you, of who you are and everything about you. These are fleeting, superficial, often quick decisions, where people decide to swipe on/unmatch/stop replying, based on many minor factors that have nothing to do with who you truly are. It might be because of hair colour, geography, liking coffee, not liking dogs ... the reality is we might not know why, but we can know for sure it *isn't and cannot* be based on truly knowing you. It is just fleeting, arbitrary decision-making – and you will do the same to a multitude of others.

So keep all this in mind about rejection. But also strengthen your resilience too. Resilience is about the ability to recover from challenges that come your way. In the case of dating, it's about being able to bounce back from someone unmatching, ghosting, not swiping. It's about being able to laugh at the silliness of this process. It's being able to say to yourself, *"If I wasn't right for that person to choose me, then they weren't right for me."*

It's about reminding yourself that there are thousands of people in the online dating world, and you don't need all of them to like you, fancy you, want to chat to you. You just need to find one that you like and who likes you back. Sometimes, yes, it will feel like trying to find a needle in a haystack. And sometimes you will need a break from the process. And sometimes it will hurt. That is understandable and okay. Give yourself time to pause if you need, then shake it off, bounce back up and try again.

Know that you can do this and you can find someone, when you are ready.

UNWANTED ATTENTION

You might not be ready to start thinking about dating just yet, but either way, it's possible that you may have experienced some unwanted attention from people making assumptions that as a single person you must be looking for love or sex. It could be you've received sexist jokes from a friend's partner or full-on advances from a married person.

Bottom line: you are allowed to speak up and tell them what they're doing or saying is wrong.

When I became a single parent, a dad of my son's friend from nursery got in touch under the guise of arranging a playdate for the kids. I thought this was a nice idea until he

225

suggested meeting me without the children or his wife. I politely refused; however, he was persistent with messaging. I told him I felt uncomfortable and blocked him on WhatsApp and Facebook. A few months later, I found a new message from him on an old Instagram account of mine. I couldn't believe he was that persistent! Again, I blocked and moved on with my life. I was torn between telling his wife or not, but as I was currently going through my own crisis, I decided to leave it; I have no idea if that was the morally correct option. What I do know, if a guy refuses to take no for an answer, he needs to get straight in the bin. **Amy**

Single-mum **Arabella** became good friends with a married dad from the school run.

"Friendship blossomed, and I didn't think twice before calling on him to help fix my son's bed. What started with friendly banter between passing the tools, turned into him grabbing my face and sticking his tongue down my throat. It was at this point we should have ended the friendship. But, we didn't. Later, a drunken night occurred, which led to a broken friendship, a shattered marriage and an awkward-as-hell school run for the next five years."

HOW TO DEAL WITH INAPPROPRIATE ATTENTION

Firstly, know this is not your fault, so don't ever let the patriarchy tell you that it is. Women receive a ridiculous amount of unwanted attention and it is not, and never will be, our fault.

1. Call them out. I know it can sometimes be scary to stand up for yourself like this, but if someone is making you

feel uncomfortable then you need to tell them. It doesn't matter if that person is your boss, your friend's husband or your neighbour. Call. Them. Out.

2. Speak out. If you've called them out and they are persistent, please tell someone. You do not have to deal with this on your own. You have every right to go to higher authorities with this.

3. Look after yourself, talk to someone, get support, be kind to yourself, don't take on blame or responsibility that isn't yours to hold.

DATING AFTER TRAUMA

Dating after you've been through heartbreak is terrifying, but dating after the trauma of an abusive relationship is a whole other ballgame. The first thing you have to do is focus on yourself; you need to heal from what has happened to you before you will be ready to move on. Therapy support can help you process the trauma, and help you move forward with healthy relationships, but be prepared for recovery from trauma to take time. Eye Movement Desensitization and Reprocessing (EMDR) is a fantastic therapy for trauma, but also counselling and talking therapies, specifically CBT for trauma or relationship-based therapies, can help too. You will need to learn and understand what a healthy relationship looks like and what are reg flags within a relationship.

It is important to trust your instincts; if you don't feel ready or you're in a situation that doesn't feel right, then go with your gut. And, finally but crucially, stay safe: always meet your dates in a public place until you feel comfortable. It is important you don't feel rushed and can go at your own pace.

THE EFFECTS OF TRAUMA

From Dr Emma: Trauma can affect us in significant ways. At its extreme it can lead to post-traumatic stress disorder (PTSD) symptoms, including flashbacks/re-experiencing, nightmares, avoidance of feared situations, and more. However, you can also experience trauma symptoms without reaching a threshold for a PTSD diagnosis.

Experiencing an abusive relationship can be traumatic and can impact on your beliefs about yourself and others, and about how relationships can be. It can also impact on your sense of safety and expectation of bad things happening. You can lose faith and trust in relationships, or may expect to be treated badly. This can leave you vulnerable during the dating process to accepting less than acceptable behaviour from a partner, or you might find it hard to trust anyone new.

If you feel you have been negatively affected by your past relationship, do take some time to process this before moving into dating again, either through therapy, self-help materials, or talking with close friends. By being aware of the way the past relationships have impacted your thoughts or behaviours, you will hopefully notice when these are triggered for you and can teach yourself to begin to respond in more healthy ways for you and, over time, for your new dating relationships.

HOPE

Dating can be tough – it can be demoralizing, soul destroying and feel like a bloody waste of time. It can also be wonderful and magical and uplifting. So, we'd like to end this chapter with a story of hope from Kelly.

Kelly *became a single mother after she escaped an abusive relationship.*

"I separated from my son's father in autumn 2016. I had a lot of support from a parenting group I was part of when my son was little. The wife in one of the couples – a friend of mine – had died six months earlier. The widowed dad and I started going on playdates as we were the only single parents in either of our friendship groups. It was all completely innocent to start with – both of us were in various states of recovery and crisis. I think, when you've been through something traumatic, you can spot it in other people and there's solidarity and kinship. Also, we had a lot of fun. It turned out we had loads in common. At that point I didn't have any interest in a relationship, I wasn't even thinking about it. But it was lovely having a new friendship, especially with another single parent who completely understood me. And to spend time with a man who was kind and decent – it helped me remember the goodness in men.

"Then, in the summer, something started to shift. In passing he called me 'Darling' by mistake. He didn't even notice, but I did, and I basically shot out the door as soon as I could reasonably excuse myself as I was freaking out a bit. Later that evening I thought 'Fuck it, I'm going to say something', so I messaged him about it. I remember waiting for his message to come back, I was very nervous. But it turned into a lovely exchange in which we both said we liked each other and maybe we should go on a date. I remember it so vividly; I was doing my son's bath time and it was so hard to focus on both things. Water everywhere, WhatsApp pinging.

"Our first date was in a local pub. I can't remember experiencing anything as sexually charged in my whole life. We were both so hyper-focused on each other, in our *own world, so aware of each other's bodies. At the end we walked out, and I remember thinking 'I won't be able to make the first move' – my self-esteem was at rock bottom after what I'd experienced in my last relationship. As we stood in front of the pub, he looked down at me and kissed me. The only way I can describe the feeling is that it felt like I was home – and it's felt like that ever since.*

"It's not the traditional love story you'd dream about – it's a bit messy, it doesn't quite go in the right order, we're always bloody knackered – but it's proper love, it's kind, it's honest, it's exciting, and it's a lot of fun."

Dating and You

Now that you've read this chapter, grab a piece of paper and go through these questions, to give yourself a better understanding of where you stand in your approach to dating right now.

1. Where are you in your readiness for dating? If you aren't ready, that's totally okay! Come back to this when you are.
2. What are you looking for from dating (when you are ready) – casual, long term, something in the middle?
3. Who are you looking, or not looking for, from dating? Don't be afraid to know what you want, but also be open to knowing this can be your opportunity to date people you may never have imagined dating before.
4. What will dating bring to your life/how will it enrich your life (if at all!)?
5. How would you like dating to fit into your life?
6. Do you need to have any conversations with your children about dating?

7. What can be fun about dating for you?
8. Have you got your "how to get out of a date/how to politely say no" lines ready? It can be fun to chat with friends about this and see what you can come up with!
9. What are the special things about you that someone will be lucky enough to discover by dating you? Shush that critical voice right now! This is all about the WOW about you.

Now, if you feel you're ready – go have fun!

10

HOW TO NAVIGATE A NEW RELATIONSHIP

You've done it, you've only gone and found someone you actually quite like! Now come a few more hurdles to jump … this parenting malarkey is anything but simple.

Finding a new relationship is such an exciting time. To enjoy the romance and the experiences of new love is wonderful. At the same time, as a mum you do need to hold both your head and your heart in mind and make wise choices to support your child and protect your bond as you navigate this process.

Whether you're introducing a new partner to your eight-month-old baby, a fully grown adult child or anything in between, it's not necessarily going to be plain sailing. As with every major life change, there will need to be some serious conversations, lots of understanding and a whole load of love! Everything you and your children are used to might be about to change, and you need to be prepared.

DECIDING WHEN SOMEONE IS RIGHT FOR YOU

How do you decide if this person is right for you, and if you are ready to take the next step of introducing to your children? Of course, everyone will have their own idea of what "right" is, but to remind yourself that you deserve the best, some things you could ask yourself include:

- Do they make you laugh, smile, giggle?
- Do they support you and empower you, encourage you and lift you up?
- Are they interested in you and your life and, of course, knowing about your child/children?
- Are they respectful of you, and of your loved ones?
- Are they kind and loving?
- Are they flexible, accommodating, able to compromise?
- Do you communicate well together?
- Do you feel you can be you, that your interests are valued, and you and your children are important to them?
- Do you have similar values, goals for life, wishes for your future?

And don't forget to watch out for red flags, such as:

- Do you have any misgivings you are trying not to notice?
- Are they controlling of what you do, say, wear?
- Do they discourage you seeing friends or family?
- Do they get cross or grumpy if you prioritize your children?
- Do they criticise you, your choices, interests, goals?
- Are they aggressive or emotionally abusive or manipulative?

INTRODUCING YOUR CHILD TO YOUR NEW PARTNER

When and how to introduce your new partner to your offspring is a tricky situation because it will be different for everyone.

Also, when you are caught in the exciting, intoxicating throes of a new relationship you may not always be thinking entirely wisely or rationally. Give yourself time to move past the exciting early days of romance, lust and fairy tales before you begin making plans that involve your child.

What is important is that you feel you and your child/children are ready to have a new partner on the scene (but keep in mind that when you are ready and when your child are ready might be two different things).

Before I introduced my son to my partner it felt like I was living two separate lives, those of "Mum Amy" and "Relationship Amy". I decided to introduce them after a couple of months. We met up at a park, and I introduced him as my friend. It was only after another couple of months that I told my son that he was actually my boyfriend. This worked well for us – it was a great way of seeing how my new partner would be around my son – and fortunately he was, indeed, an absolute dream. **Amy**

Frankie *introduced her daughter to her new boyfriend after she had only been seeing him for a few weeks, but described him as a friend.*

"I introduced him when I did for a few reasons. One: we were both older and had been really open about the fact we were looking for long-term relationships, and I didn't feel he would mess me around. Also, Luna was only just coming up to three, so her comprehension wasn't the same had she been older."

While Frankie and Amy both introduced their children when the relationships were fairly new, you might prefer to wait a while before taking the jump. There are a number of things to consider that may impact on your decision.

- How serious are you about this relationship?
- Have you given yourself time to make sure you really know your new partner and how the relationship will work? Give the relationship time to settle, and for both of you to stop being on your best behaviour (as we all are at the start of a relationship), to really see how you are together.
- How long was your relationship with your child's other parent? Consider how attached your child may be to the idea of you being with your ex-partner rather than someone new.
- What is the timing between the break-up from your child's other parent and your new relationship? Do you or your child need more time to process this loss first?
- How old are your children? Young children may be fairly oblivious to you having or needing a dating life, whereas older teens or adult children may be very aware, in which case being open and honest is the best way forward while still being mindful of their mental health and adjustment in this process.
- What is your child's developmental level and understanding of relationships, or of your need or readiness to date?
- How is your child's mental health and adjustment in relation to the family changes?
- How do your children cope with meeting new people? Have they experienced meeting their other parent's new partner? Do they know other families with step-parents?
- How much child-free time do you have? If you can, it may be best to enjoy the dating time child-free for as long

as possible to give you time to really get to know this relationship.

• Do you need to rush this introduction? If this is a relationship for the long term, can you take your time?

Keep in mind your child/children may have a range of thoughts and feelings about you dating and finding a new partner. Introducing someone new is likely to be unsettling even in the best of circumstances. Wherever possible, be sensitive to this, giving your child the space and time to express and process how they are thinking and feeling. It is understandable they may be experiencing all sorts of emotions or responses. Seeing their parent find someone new can be a situation a child is okay with, but equally can be very upsetting for them. Try to be attuned to this and support them with how they feel. Sometimes it can help to voice this for them; for example, "I can imagine it might feel a bit strange/rubbish/sad, talking about me having a new boyfriend. Is that how it feels?"

Overall there is not a right or wrong answer for when you should introduce your new relationship to your child, it is what works best for you and your family at the time.

> **Katie's** ex-partner met someone new a year after they separated. She asked him to wait a year before introducing his new partner to the children.
>
> "I knew my children (both primary school age) were still sad about the break-up of our relationship and I didn't feel it was necessary for them to go through this new meeting yet. I also knew I wasn't ready for this next step, and I wanted to be able to support it. So we waited until they had been together a year and then went ahead."

There might also be reasons that make you feel wary or uncomfortable about opening your family up to a new person;

for example, past trauma and abuse can make it incredibly difficult to open up or bring someone new into your solo family. If this is your experience, give yourself time, but also seek therapy support if you need.

> **Bree Ann** struggled to trust her new partner after she suffered from an abusive relationship and sexual abuse.
> "Up until a few years ago, I did not leave my daughter alone with my new partner. Through therapy and open conversations I started to feel more comfortable, and now he sees her as his daughter and treats her as such."

TIPS FOR INTRODUCING YOUR CHILD TO SOMEONE NEW

Ultimately, take it slow – make sure *both* you and your new partner feel ready. And, if you have an amicable relationship, it is good to check in with your ex-partner to see how they feel about it too (especially, if you would appreciate them showing you the same courtesy).

Tips for those with younger children:

- Tell your child before they meet – you can say it's a friend or special friend you'd like them to meet.
- Take your time (weeks or months) before explaining they are a boyfriend or girlfriend.
- Initially meet in a neutral location, like a park.
- Reassure your child – make sure they know that they are still your number one priority.
- Be patient with them – it might take them a while before feeling comfortable with a new person.
- Try not to start including your new partner in every occasion with your child. Go slow with future meetings – take your time, for you and your child.

Tips for those with teenagers/adult children (some of this may apply to pre-teen and early teens too; you will know what's best for your child).

- Take it slow, as above.
- Talk to your teenager/adult child – find out how they are doing in relation to the family changes. Let them be open and honest. Listen and be empathic to their experiences.
- Be gentle and honest with them about being ready to date again and meeting someone you like. Let them know this doesn't take away from the role their other parent has, and is not about replacing anyone – this is just something for you.
- Let them know you'd like them to meet when they are ready. Let them choose the timing and location – do they want to meet on a walk, do they want to go for dinner, have a drink in the pub?
- Keep it time limited for first meetings. Go slow.
- Be patient as above.

Take your time with each stage of the process. Go slow to help all of you adjust. If this relationship is for the long term, you have the time. Stages may include: introducing your partner, being present for days out, having them spend time at the house, having them spend the night at your house, spending holidays together, and of course moving in.

MOVING BACK INTO A PARTNERSHIP

You've gone through all the challenges of becoming a single mum – you've worked through the emotional challenge, have found your place and settled into the journey; you have developed your independence, skills, habits and maybe even a confidence you could never have imagined possible … and then you met someone who makes you feel ready for a relationship all over again.

This can feel amazing, wonderful, exciting, incredible, but it does means you have to open yourself up to being in a partnership again. You and your children have to be willing to accommodate someone else's routines and habits (and they, yours). These changes can be unsettling for both you and your children, and it may take time to figure it all out. It's okay.

It is important to protect your time with both your new relationship and with your child. You can do this by planning date nights on your child-free days and planning special one-to-one time with your child. Concentrate on making sure you don't change the routines for your child/children or your role too much or too quickly. If anything, give your child that extra special attention so they know they are your priority.

If your child does react negatively to your new partner, be careful not to get into conflict or reject/punish them. Take the time to sit down and talk about how they are doing with everything. Let them know you can sense they are unhappy, or feeling angry. Hear what they have to say. Let them know you are always there to talk with them and to figure things out together. Know that even though it is hard for you, it is okay for them to feel angry, or have a negative response, and validating how they feel is essential. It doesn't mean you stop seeing your partner, (unless they have behaved in a way that is a clear red flag that absolutely justifies your child's response), but you can slow things down between them and your child until your child is more ready.

Try to keep communicating, letting your child talk, and letting them know they will always be your priority. Let them hear that and let them see and feel that through your actions too. It is important to check out how they are thinking and feeling at each stage of the process.

Maintaining Your Special Relationship with Your Child

When a new partner enters your little solo-parent dynamic, it can be unsettling for you and your child/children. Taking some time to support and prioritize your relationship with your child will be helpful for all of you.

1. Acknowledge change is unsettling and that it will take time for you all to get used to it.
2. Talk about what is really important for both of you to protect in your life – it might be you have routines that you or the children really want to keep in place just for you and them.
3. Chat about something you can do together every week that will be just yours – a playdate, dinner out, swimming, a movie night, a pamper evening, or just playing footie in the park after school.
4. Make a list of the special plans you can create or keep in place.
5. Make sure you get ideas from your child of what they want or would like.

ADAPTING YOUR INDEPENDENCE

Being in a partnership will also mean letting go of, or at least creating some shift in, your newfound independence – and this may feel tough, even a little scary. Try to figure this out together with your partner.

Be honest about where you are finding it tough. Communication, openness and flexibility will be key here. As a highly independent person, allowing another person to slot into your family life can be pretty daunting. It can also be pretty darn fantastic – having support from an adult human can turn those tough, lonely nights around.

NAVIGATING THE NEW DYNAMIC

Once you've decided that your new relationship is serious and you've introduced them to the children, the next step to navigate is how you, your partner and your ex-partner can all work together to benefit you all and your children. There are different hurdles or changes you may have to navigate here.

YOUR NEW PARTNER AND YOUR EX-PARTNER'S RELATIONSHIP

Depending on the situation and the relationship you have with your ex-partner, you may find yourself having to navigate how your new partner and ex-partner get on. For some, there may be no contact at all; others may develop a relationship that is civil or even friendly!

This can be a strange process for you, your new partner and your ex-partner, and it is important to give yourself time to process whatever emotions this brings up, while remembering that if everyone can get on this is actually a wonderful thing for your child.

It can, of course, be challenging if your new and ex-partner don't get on, or there is jealousy, conflict or aggression. If this is the case, where possible try to appeal to both of them to be calm and civil for the sake of your child. If your new partner is not able to do this it is a red flag, as this type of conflict will not help anyone. If your ex-partner is driving the conflict and won't work with you to calm the situation, you may need to set boundaries in place to minimize or remove all contact between the two.

SURVIVING SOLO MOTHERHOOD

IMPACT ON THE RELATIONSHIP BETWEEN YOUR EX-PARTNER AND YOUR CHILD

If your ex-partner and child/children have a really strong relationship, then bringing a new partner into the situation will likely have little impact. However, where perhaps the relationship isn't as strong, it can sometimes lead to changes in their relationship. Sometimes there may be a correlation between bringing a new partner into the child's life and the biological parent becoming more involved and communicative. While this improvement in relations may have been triggered by dubious reasons, this can nevertheless be great news for your child.

> **Clare's** new relationship had the impact of improving her son's relationship with his dad.
> "My partner treats my son as his own and they get on amazingly well. It's been really good for my son to have a really stable and positive male figure in his life. It's also made his dad step up a bit more and be more present with his son, as he hasn't always been that reliable. I feel so lucky that things have worked out so well for us all; it felt at the time like it could go the other way, but we've all worked hard to get to where we are now, and it's really paid off."

Watching your child form a bond with a new partner is so lovely to see, and even lovelier when they can still have a bond with their other parent too.

AGREEING ON PARENTING AND CO-PARENTING

Co-parenting isn't a walk in the park, and involving new partners in that scene can be tricky. When Amy's ex got into a new relationship, she was worried about the new partner taking on a motherly role.

> *I took the time to talk to her, and was reassured that she did not want to step on anyone's toes and would be leaving all things like disciplining to my ex. I felt quite lucky, as my feelings had been taken into account and my ex and his new partner were doing what's best for Milo.* **Amy**

Nevertheless, there will be some new partners who have thoughts and ideas about how the step parenting or co-parenting should be. Or it could be that you or your ex-partner may be unhappy with how your or their new partner is with your child. When this happens it is tricky because you are then having to balance what's best for your child with the emotions and feelings of other adults.

While you will need to take your new partner's feelings into account, you also need to make sure whatever you do isn't unnecessarily jeopardizing your co-parenting relationship, for your child's sake.

You may want to set out with your new partner in advance how and why you do things with your ex, and to ask for their support with your decisions around this. If your new partner does raise concerns about the co-parenting between you and your ex, take the time to listen to these concerns, talk them through (away from your child), and also take time for yourself to reflect on what you think is best for your child.

There may be times when it is quite right to continue doing things as you have been doing them up to now, and there may also be times when your new partner highlights some helpful new ideas that you could chat to your ex-partner about introducing. Try to make this process as open and collaborative as possible. Both you and your ex-partner may struggle with someone new coming in and suggesting new ways of doing things, and it is okay to give everyone time to think this through and not rush into new ways. There is also a difference between your new partner offering helpful new ideas, and being critical of how you and your ex-partner are doing things and expecting you to change without question. The first can be encouraged, the latter is more problematic and a potential red flag.

You may also want to talk through with your new partner about how you would like them to be involved in parenting or not. Be open to exploring your ideas and what your new partner is comfortable with. This may be different for everyone and may depend on many factors, including your child, how old they are and the support they need. Some single parents are happy for a new partner to be involved in homework, discipline, bedtime, etc, while others may feel very strongly that they don't want this involvement from their new partner. You may also have differences in parenting methods, which you will need to think about and talk through in advance. Ideally your new partner will respect the methods you choose with your child.

For more reading on co-parenting, including navigating a new partner, we recommend *The Co-Parenting Handbook* by Karen Bonnell.

STORIES OF NEW RELATIONSHIPS FROM SINGLE MOTHERHOOD

Once you have found your new partner, it is okay to know that you can make this work for you any way you like. Some people want to move in together as soon as it feels right, while others prefer to maintain separate homes and separate family lives, and to spend time together when they are both free from parenting. There is no right or wrong way, it is just about finding what works for you both.

Emilia *and her partner both have teenage children.*

"My boyfriend and I have been together for three years and both have teenage children, and different routines/commitments with our childcare. The children are all at that teenage age that is a bit awkward; they don't really know each other or have things in common, and it is stressful trying to make them all do things together. So we have settled on a routine that means we spend our time with our children separately, and are together when we have time to ourselves. We have our separate houses and that works for us."

Dani *found a new partner when she was in her 50s.*

"My new partner and I bought a place together and he lived with me and my children. However his older teenage son wasn't keen to be part of this, so he lived separately with his mum and chose not to be part of our blended family. This was stressful sometimes, but we respected his choices and supported him to have a good relationship with his dad in their own time."

Frenchie *introduced her new boyfriend to her son. However, they don't see each other consistently due to work and school.*

"I like to have one-on-one time with my son and then be carefree and in my twenties again with my boyfriend (I'm still 27, but parenting has aged me in dog years!). When the two lives combine, I feel a bit torn in two. Over the last few years, I've got so used to being independent that I struggle to understand how I'm supposed to live in some level of harmony with more than just my son."

Jessica's experience was different again.

"My (now) fiancé and I both had children from our previous relationships. We introduced them slowly. They were all under 12 and got on surprisingly well, considering. We moved in together after two years, and have lived together ever since. It's pretty busy with them coming and going. They all go to their mum's or dad's at different times or days, so sometimes we have them all here and sometimes none of them are here, and any combination in between!"

BLENDED FAMILIES

If you and your new partner eventually move in together, you will be looking at how to navigate creating a blended family. This might be creating the new family with your partner and your children, or introducing your partner's children into the home, or having a child of your own together.

Bringing other children into your family dynamic might seem like a challenge, and it is going to be a massive learning curve for everyone involved – including the kids. You and your new partner may need to set up a (work in progress) plan from the very beginning. Every situation is so personal, so it is important that everyone involved is happy with the boundaries set.

TIPS FOR BLENDING YOUR FAMILIES

- Follow all our tips on slowly introducing a new partner.
- Take your time before moving in and blending the families. This requires planning, and if this is forever there is no rush. Doing this sensitively and carefully is most important for everyone's mental health and success.

- Keep your ex-partner updated on the process where possible.
- Take your time planning how to introduce your new partner's children to yours.
- Talk to your child/children about this process before it happens – explore their thoughts and feelings.
- Introduce new children slowly, in the same way as a new partner. Again start in a neutral place, for example, the park or on a lunch date.
- Think about the situation from the children's point of view and go easy with them. It's going to take them time to adjust, so don't expect them to be best buddies with your partner's kids straight away. In fact, they just might not get on. Just because you and their parent are in a relationship doesn't mean they will magically connect as well. Be prepared for this.
- Remember they may also be feeling sad, scared, jealous, worried. They may be super excited too, so don't assume anything. Just be prepared for this experience to take time and to bring up a lot of thoughts and feelings for both your and your partner's children.
- Take time to think with your partner about how living together will work. What do your kids need and what do your partner's kids need? What routines and home comforts are important? How can you accommodate these for everyone?
- Make sure both you and your partner have one-on-one time with your kids.
- Organize family activities everyone will enjoy – a trip to the cinema, the beach or even playing a video game together.
- Work on your co-parenting relationship with your ex and encourage your new partner to do the same.
- Agree on a plan for disciplining.

It can be best for your new partner to let you take the lead on disciplining, especially at first, as it can be difficult for a child to accept this from a new partner. If, however, you do agree to share the responsibility of disciplining (perhaps over time), then it's important that your new partner's views regarding discipline align with your own.

Isabel *invited a new partner, and his children, into her life and found he appeared to be stricter with her children than his own.*

"After discussing the situation, we realized it was because he was worried about upsetting his kids as he only gets to see them once a fortnight. We have worked together to set rules we can all live with, and he has become more aware of treating the children differently. He has also asked that I discipline his children the same way I would mine."

Allison's *new partner didn't have any children of her own, and her views on parenting were very different to Allison's.*

"When we all moved in together, I found myself playing the peacemaker between my girlfriend and six-year-old son. Inevitably, this relationship didn't work out. I couldn't keep being the 'in between' for my son and my girlfriend, it made me feel like I had to pick sides, and obviously I would always side with my son."

For *Frankie*, *to begin with, her partner left the disciplining to her. However, when they had a baby together it felt strange to be then splitting the disciplining.*

"Now, he will discipline if necessary, but he always follows my way of doing it. If I am around, he will often call me in to discuss the issue rather than be the one to issue discipline himself. As long as he follows my way of parenting, I am happy for him to be fully involved. He has *been with her since she was small, and now we have a child together it just makes sense."*

> *My partner didn't discipline my son; however he did have a short temper when my son was being difficult. There were countless times I had to remind him that it was just a kid being a kid. My way of parenting is very gentle – I like to discuss why my son is playing up and try to talk out the problems rather than shouting and disciplining, whereas because my partner had grown up in quite a strict household, his views on parenting didn't quite align with mine.* **Amy**

WHAT IF THINGS GO WRONG?

Adding an extra person into your family is bound to change the dynamic of your household. And, as Amy found out, if the new relationship then doesn't work out, it can be a tricky thing to handle with your children.

> *As my new partner spent more time with both my son and me, life felt like it was flowing in a lovely direction. My son adored him, and he did his best to play a step-fatherly type figure. The problem with love is it's so unpredictable, I found myself planning a new life with this man, then after 18 months the commitment was too much for him – "See ya". This heartbreak wasn't devastating for me – I'd survived the last one and I sure as hell was going to survive this one. What was devastating was the thought of having to tell my son – who had seen this man as a role model – that we had broken up. I took a few weeks to get over the heartbreak myself, then I told him one evening that we had broken up*

> *and would stay friends. My son took it pretty well; however, we did have a replay of some of the questions he asked when his dad first left. This was obviously very upsetting, and I do worry that he might feel like he's been abandoned.*
> **Amy**

TIPS FOR TALKING TO A CHILD ABOUT A BREAK-UP

- Be honest – tell them it didn't work out.
- Try to keep it light – focus on the fact you can still be friends (even if this doesn't come to fruition).
- Don't discourage them when they want to talk to you about it – it might be tough for you, but it is okay for them to want to talk or ask questions about why this person isn't in their life anymore.

WHEN EVERYTHING WORKS OUT

You've been through single motherhood, you've taken those steps into dating, you've found an incredible new partner, whether you were really looking for them or not, and you've successfully blended your family to include them. And things are looking really, really lovely.

So, let yourself enjoy the company, the romance, the love and care. Let yourself offer this too. Trust in your new partner, value what they bring to your life, and what you bring to theirs, and also remember you can always be you. Everything you have learnt as a single mum you can bring to this new relationship.

Take care of each other and your new family. Be kind, be loving. Be accepting and forgiving. Go on date nights. Enjoy family time. Create new traditions. Practise self-care and self-development. Let yourself enjoy this.

Ultimately, none of us know what the future is going to hold, so don't forget to take the time to just enjoy this newfound love – you blimmin' well deserve to! Take all the time you need for yourself and your kids, and we're sure you'll do a grand job for you and your family. You've got this!

11

FINDING YOU

POSITIVE MENTAL HEALTH AND EMBRACING SINGLE MOTHERHOOD

Amazing job – you've found your way through this book to our last chapter, where we really want to focus completely on YOU. You and your wellbeing. Being a single mum is an incredible, tough, empowering, scary, overwhelming, exhausting, freeing experience. We've talked through the challenges, the ways our mental health can be affected, the rollercoaster of finding our power, our joy, maybe dating and even a new relationship when you are ready. And for this last chapter we want to focus on how to help you find your wellbeing, your positive mental health, on your journey surviving *and thriving* in solo motherhood.

TEN KEY WAYS TO LOOK AFTER YOUR MENTAL HEALTH

Below we've shared ten key ways to look after yourself and your mental health. We hope you find these helpful and empowering. Treat them as useful nudges to help you take some steps today to look after yourself a little more – after all, you deserve this.

1. EAT WELL

One cannot think well, love well, sleep well, if one has not dined well.

Virginia Woolf, author and poet

Eating well is so important for our energy levels, physical health and mood. However, being a single mum is relentless, and often finding time to stop and eat well can feel like an impossible task. It's easy to end up missing breakfast, lunch being on the go and dinner being the kids' leftovers, takeaway, cereal, toast or chocolate as you are just too tired for anything else. Plus, cooking for one (if you and the kids aren't eating the same meals) can be a bit soul destroying at first.

You may also be conscious of your weight, as most of us are. You might be trying to lose weight, or trying to put some weight back on if you have been struggling to eat due to the stress. On top of that, shopping with your children can be really stressful as a single mum. You might have been able to sneak off to the stores child-free before you became a single mum, and now you are faced with having to manage the supermarket with kids while you attempt the big shop. No fun for anyone!

Whatever your situation, trying to find ways to eat well can easily end up at the bottom of the priority list as a single mum. If you have actually already got yourself in a great routine of eating well as a single mum, then brilliant, please keep it up, and you can move on to the next wellbeing tip. If not, we hope the following ideas will be helpful.

- Remind yourself you deserve to eat well.
- Be kind to yourself, adjusting to cooking for one is hard. It's okay if sometimes you eat beans on toast, but try not

to let it become a regular routine. Value yourself enough to make substantial meals.

- Make a meal plan for the week and plan your shop in advance. Setting regular days for doing an online food shop and delivery helps with the organization of this and makes it easier to make sure you have what you need.
- See if you can get milk delivered. It can be a lifesaver getting regular milk and bread/eggs delivered.
- Try batch cooking – make up a big pot of food on a Sunday evening and freeze portions. If you are eating just for you, having a portion of homecooked food ready to defrost and heat up can really help rather than cooking a solo meal every evening.
- Make a list of quick and easy meals for when you are feeling tired and worn down; ask friends or family for ideas and inspiration.
- Involve the kids in cooking with you; learning how to prepare and cook food are valuable skills, and it makes it more interactive and companionable for you.
- Embrace the pleasure of knowing you get to choose the meals you are having each day without having to accommodate anyone else's preferences (apart from your children's if you are all eating together!). You can also encourage your children to try new foods with you, which will be great for them.

2. GET SOME SLEEP

Sleep is the single most effective thing we can do to reset our brain and body health each day.

Professor Matthew Walker, *Why We Sleep: Unlocking the Power of Sleep and Dreams*

The power that sleep has for our physical and mental health cannot be *overestimated*. If you want an in-depth understanding of this, listen to Professor Matthew Walker on Dr Rangan Chatterjee's podcast (drchatterjee.com) talking about why sleep is the most important pillar of health. In a nutshell, good sleep can help improve our health, reduce our chance of illness, improve our memory, help weight loss, improve mood, and more.

Of course, as a single mum, sleep can easily be disrupted. This might be because of your children waking; going to bed late and getting up early for work, house and parenting duties; or stress, anxiety, worry, trauma and depression keeping you awake.

If you are struggling with sleep we hope the following ideas will be helpful.

- Value your sleep, protect your sleep time. The benefits of sleep are so numerous, so don't under prioritize it.
- Implement a regular sleep pattern: a regular bedtime and – regardless of how you have slept – a regular wake-up time.
- Establish a "wind down for bed" routine; this helps signal to your mind and body it is getting ready for sleep. This could be having a warm drink, brushing your teeth, moisturizing, reading, and then trying to sleep once sleepy.
- Make your bedroom conducive to sleep with a good mattress and nice bedding, a dim or dark environment, a comfortable temperature. Also, try to keep it tidy, and don't use your bedroom for work if you can – only use it for sleep, reading/tv or sex!
- Try to limit your screen time before bed. The blue light acts a stimulant and can disrupt sleep patterns. If you can, pop your phone on the side out of reach in your bedroom, or even better keep it out of the bedroom altogether.

- There are some lovely products these days that can aid sleep, such as pillow sprays (try those from This Works), sleep masks to induce calm and wellbeing (Spacemasks are highly recommended) and weighted blankets (often used to reduce anxiety). Sleep aids like these are a bit of a treat, but can be really worth it for that peaceful night's sleep.
- Meditation apps, such as Calm and Headspace, have some sleep meditations to listen to as you lie in bed. If you use these on your phone, turn the phone face down so you don't see the screen. For children there is a lovely guided meditation on YouTube called "The Secret Treehouse" by New Horizon.
- Use any of the sleep strategies from Chapter 5 Anxiety for managing worries or negative thoughts at night.
- If your children wake you up, do what you need to help them sleep again as soon as possible, and know these phases will pass. Do what works best for you and your family; some of us will and some of us won't be happy to bring children into our beds – there is no right or wrong way. Your children will learn to sleep in their own beds with time, so do not stress about this.

3. MOVE YOUR BODY

Move your body because you can.

Amanda Kloots, TV personality

Exercise is important to both our physical and mental health. Beyond improving your fitness or how your body looks, research has shown exercise can lift mood, improve sleep, increase energy and motivation, improve memory and attention, improve problem-solving skills, help with decision-making, enhance self-esteem, and increase confidence. Exercise is a one-stop-shop for lifting us up. Of course, it isn't a magic wand – it doesn't make life challenges go away – and it also works best when you can believe in it and find a form of exercise that you love.

> For **Emilia**, exercise has been a joy that has come into her life as a single mum.
>   "Becoming a single mum is really tough at times, but in a way, it is an opportunity to become your own best friend. For me, exercise has helped to build inner confidence. I know it's just a body, but feeling strong and healthy is so empowering and has definitely helped me feel more able to deal with whatever comes my way."

If you are open to giving exercise and moving more a go, here are some ideas you might find helpful.

- Anyone can exercise – ANYONE. Even if you have never exercised before, you can still find something that works for you. Of course, if you aren't sure about your own physical situation, do seek medical or professional advice first.
- Finding ways to move your body and keep fit will help you have the energy to keep up with your children.
- Exercise can be fun, particularly when you find something you love, and there are so many different ways you can exercise: walk, jog, skip, jump, dance, hit the gym, lift weights, box, cycle, spin, do yoga, Pilates, paddleboard, skateboard, ski, surf, swim, play sport.
- Just moving more is a great start, so start with trying to walk more. Or put on your favourite playlist and dance around your kitchen!
- You can start slowly and build up.
- Finding a friend who can be a training buddy can be great, or you can explore getting a trainer or try an online fitness programme.

- Fitting exercise into your life may need a bit of organization or discipline. Find a way that works for you, and don't beat yourself up about what you can't do. If once a week is all you can fit in, this is fine to start.
- If you are a morning person, see if you can sneak in a workout before the kids get up; if you are an evening person, see if you can do a workout after bedtime or if you can ask for an hour's childcare from friends, family or your ex-partner. Alternatively, allow your children half an hour on a screen while you exercise, and don't feel guilty about this.
- See if you and your kids can work out together at home or at the park, or involve them by getting them to time you or count the number of exercises.
- If working out in the week feels impossible, then don't beat yourself up; try looking for a time at the weekend that might work. If it still feels too tricky, a family walk is a good start.
- If it's hard to get out and exercise, there are some great free online activities: "Yoga by Adrienne" is on YouTube; "Skipping with Sarah" is on Instagram; Ryan Heffington on Instagram does some great Ibiza-style dance videos; Joe Wicks' HIIT workouts are on YouTube; or seek out "Couch to 5K" running programmes.

4. ACCEPT HELP

Accepting help is its own kind of strength.

Keira Cass, writer

This one is short and simple, so don't overthink it: being a single mum is really bloomin' tough, so don't be afraid to accept or ask for help.

You could start by creating various WhatsApp groups with those who you can call on for help, whether it's for school pick-ups, playdates, cover for an hour so you can pop to the gym or do the shopping, or childcare weekends with the grandparents.

Accepting help does not mean you are failing as a parent. Rather, it will enable you to cope with the challenges single parenthood brings. Unfortunately, you aren't *actually* a superwoman, even though you absolutely deserve that title! Everyone has their limits, so accept help and give yourself a break.

5. SELF-CARE ISN'T SELFISH

As important as it is to have a plan for doing work,
it is perhaps more important to have a plan for rest,
relaxation, self-care, and sleep.

Akiroq Brost, writer

Self-care is one of those buzz words you have probably heard used a lot, but what are we really talking about? Self-care is anything you can do to look after *you*, anything that helps you rest, recharge, re-energize, calm, soothe. Incorporating self-care into your life means giving yourself the chance to look after you and, by doing so, enabling you to be the best you can be, as a mum and as yourself.

It can be easy as a single mother to just run yourself into the ground, but there are no prizes for this. If you burn out physically or mentally, you will be no good for yourself, your children, your work, your friends, any new partner. So, finding time for self-care is important.

Jemma explained:
"I have always been an on-the-go person. I spend my time rushing around from task to task, and part of me really

likes that. But one of the things that has helped me the most in the past couple of years is telling myself it is okay to stop, to do really nice things for me. I sometimes give myself permission to get into bed early and binge watch my favourite series. Or I take a long bath while the kids are on screens. I also treated myself to some really nice shower products and a shower radio; I play really fun songs in the shower to lift me up in the morning. I love it! It's my five minutes of self-care."

Self-care will be individual to you – it's about what helps *you* feel rested, soothed, calmed, re-energized – and it could look like any of the following.

- Give yourself a night/day/weekend off – and enjoy it! Taking time off, but then beating yourself up the whole time for what else you should be doing isn't self-care!
- Pamper yourself with anything from a warm bath to a massage, a manicure/pedicure or a trip to the hairdressers.
- Breathe and meditate – make time to regularly practise slow, deep breathing exercises or meditation practices.
- Enact self-care through simple daily activities: eat well, brush your teeth, shower, wear nice clothes, drink enough water.
- Treat yourself – buy yourself flowers, your favourite coffee, cake, moisturizer, a new book.
- Get outside – be in nature, go for a walk, spend time in the garden, visit a beauty spot, spend time near water – anywhere that brings you a sense of peace or rest or enjoyment.
- Take time to exercise if you know it helps you feel good.
- Say "No" – set boundaries, turn your computer off, pace the amount of tasks or activities you take on.

- Take time to read, listen to music, dance, listen to a podcast, paint, draw, etc.
- Be kind and compassionate to yourself.

6. TALK

There is no greater agony than bearing an untold story inside you.

Maya Angelou, author

Keep talking – whether it's with friends, family or in therapy. It is so healthy to talk to others about how you are doing and, of course, about them too. There is so much that can be gained from a thoughtful conversation with someone you trust. Never underestimate the power of a helpful comment from a friend that you can reflect on and learn from. Never underestimate the power of being able to talk and process through how you are thinking and feeling. This is always more helpful than keeping things bottled up or shut away.

Of course, while talking to friends can be really helpful, do keep in mind that you don't overburden them (as, realistically, this can happen). You can solve this by either developing a friendship circle of people you can chat to at different times (see Find Your People – tip 8) or you can seek support through therapy. Using therapy is not a sign of failure or weakness – it is a sign of strength and bravery to reach out for support when it is needed. Therapy can help us to express our thoughts and feelings and understand what we are going through, and it can help us to learn new ways of coping with and responding to difficult situations. See Chapter 5 for more details about different therapies and their benefits, and below for a quick summary of your options for therapy.

- Seek out private (self-funded or funded via health insurance) or state-supported therapy options; some charities also offer free or low-cost therapy options.
- Choose a type of therapy (for example, EMDR therapy, CBT, ACT, family therapy, couple therapy, psychodynamic therapy, etc) and a professional (counsellor, CBT therapist, clinical psychologist, counselling psychologist, psychodynamic psychotherapist, systemic therapist, etc.) that suits you (there are many types of therapy and therapy professionals).
- Decide whether you are looking for something short-term or long-term, as different therapy professionals and therapy models have different approaches according to your choice.

7. LEARN SOMETHING NEW

Learn something new. Try something different. Convince yourself every day that you have no limits.

Brian Tracy, writer and motivational speaker

Doing something that we can gain a sense of achievement from can do wonders for our mental health. After becoming a single parent, we can feel a little lost and there may be activities and routines that have had to change, whether you like it or not. So, finding a new or rekindling an old hobby or pastime can be good for your confidence and give you something to focus on and enjoy. Some ideas could include:

- Learn to cook or bake.
- Join a sports club or team – tennis, football, hockey, rugby.
- Learn a new activity – paddleboarding, chess.
- Learn a music instrument – piano, guitar, drums.

- Teach yourself DIY or gardening.
- Get creative – draw, paint, sculpt, knit, crochet, sew.
- Learn a new language.
- Become a runner, weightlifter, cyclist, swimmer.

Katie agrees with this.

"I took up paddleboarding after I became a single parent. Luckily, I had a friend who had some paddleboards and we just went out and had a go together. I think I was only able to do this because I had got into exercise massively, which increased my confidence and my readiness to give new challenges a go. I was really chuffed I was able to master it. Being on the water is so peaceful and soothing after a long day at work. I'd recommend it to anyone!"

8. FIND YOUR PEOPLE

You can't stay in your corner of the Forest waiting for others to come to you. You have to go to them sometimes.

A.A. Milne, *Winnie-the-Pooh*

Becoming a single parent is difficult for many reasons, and one challenge can be finding your way socially. We have talked about grieving the loss and companionship of the relationship with your ex-partner, and about changes socially if friends actively choose a "side" between you and your ex-partner or you no longer feel comfortable going to couple or family events anymore.

So building up the people and connections you have that you can turn to, and building a new social life for you as a single parent, can really help your wellbeing. This might be easy for those whose friendships have remained pretty much the same, but for others it might take more work. Whichever, it is absolutely worth focusing on, as we thrive so much on the social connections, friendships and support around us. If you are finding this tricky, we hope the following ideas will be helpful.

- Have a go at the Friendship Tree task on page 17, to sketch out the people in your life who are important to you. Go through your phone or your Facebook profile as a prompt to remind yourself, and include casual friends who you might message only occasionally, as well as people you would go on holiday with or hang out with every week. All these friends can have their place, and you will soon realize that there are probably more people to draw on your friendship tree than you first thought.
- Learn to recognize the friends that build you up and support you and the ones who make you feel less good – focus on those who make you feel great.
- Know that friendships may change as a single parent; life challenges such as separation and divorce always bring about changes. Go with the process and allow yourself to process your sadness or frustrations for the friends who fall by the wayside.
- Be open to building up new connections by meeting new people, making new school mum friends, or joining a new club or app to meet a new social group. Be brave, have a go.
- Be open to being more assertive in initiating plans and activities. You are living a new life and a new routine now, and people may need time to adjust to this. You may also be the one with more commitments or specific routines, so take the lead in making plans for your child-free days or with your child on days when they are with you. Don't be afraid to be the one to reach out for the coffee date, wine date, playdate. The worst that can happen is

others are busy and say no, but it is likely you will get a favourable response.

• Build up meaningful connections through messaging, meeting up, supporting each other – accept help and offer help.

9. PRACTISE SELF-ACCEPTANCE AND SELF-COMPASSION

Self-acceptance is perhaps the best gift you can give yourself. Self-acceptance is without condition; it means that you accept yourself as is, flaws and all.

Heather Lonczak, PhD, psychologist, writer and poet

Self-compassion is simply giving the same kindness to ourselves that we give to others ... Self-compassion soothes the mind like a loving friend who's willing to listen to your difficulties without giving advice.

Christopher Germer, clinical psychologist

The journey to single motherhood can be full of heavy thoughts and feelings, sadness, regret, shame, self-criticism, self-judgement. You may lie awake wishing a million things were different – in yourself, in your life, in your family. And one of the most powerful antidotes we can offer for all of this is to practise self-acceptance and self-compassion.

Self-acceptance is about accepting you for who you are. You aren't perfect – no one is. You are flawed, which is part of being human. You have areas of strength, and areas where you don't flourish as much. You will look in the mirror and see wobbly bits, stretched bits, wrinkly bits – EVERYBODY does. You may have had moments in your life you wish hadn't happened, that you would go back and change if you could. Again, this is normal.

Self-acceptance is acknowledging *all* of these things and saying, "I'm okay. I'm enough. I'm good enough. I'm flawed, but I am amazing. I accept this is me and where I am right now. It doesn't mean that I can't choose to focus on change in the future. I can still choose to improve my fitness, to work on self-improvement with my external skills or internal habits. I can try to be more thoughtful, and practise more kindness."

Self-compassion is about being as kind and compassionate to yourself as you are to your loved ones. Self-compassion means talking to yourself kindly, treating yourself kindly. It means less of the inner bully, the inner critic, and more of the inner nurturer, the inner carer, the friend.

A key benefit of self-compassion is that we are more likely to succeed and reach our goals by practising self-compassion than by being self-critical and judgemental toward ourselves.

So, take some time to see if you can practise self-acceptance and self-compassion today, perhaps with some of the following examples of compassionate self-talk.

- Stand in front of the mirror, take in what you see, and gently say to yourself, "This is me, this is me as I am today, the me I have become through everything I have been through. I am not perfect and that is okay. No one is. I can learn to accept myself, the bits I love and the bits I am not so sure of. I can learn to accept these are me and I am grateful for me and my body."
- When something challenging happens or difficult emotions are triggered, tell yourself: "This is hard right now, this is painful. I am struggling with this. I can be kind to myself through this, I can listen to what I need."
- When you make a mistake, acknowledge it and accept it by saying to yourself, "I feel terrible for this mistake. I feel

sadness/pain for the people this has hurt. I know this was a mistake and I didn't intend this, and I am doing my best to figure this out."

- When you are struggling with depression, anxiety, guilt, shame as a single parent, tell yourself: "I feel really sad/guilty/low/anxious/shameful right now. It is really tough being a single parent and trying to cope with all the emotions it brings. These emotions are understandable in the situation I am in. I am doing what I can to find a way through this. I can send myself love and kindness right now."
- Practise the Kind Hands exercise from page 83.
- At any point, if you feel low, remind yourself: "It's tough right now. I can do something nice and kind for myself right now. I can take some time to make myself a cup of tea, buy myself some flowers, cuddle my dog, snuggle with my child, put on my favourite music, cook my favourite food, give myself a break."

10. EMBRACE YOUR NEW SOLO-PARENT FAMILY

Be who you are, and find yourself so you can be your own person and enjoy life with no regret.

Bonnie Zackson Koury, writer

We want to finish with some important thoughts about helping you reach a place where you can really find *you* again, and also find meaning and joy in your solo-motherhood family. You will find this place, we promise, even if it feels impossible to ever imagine reaching a place where you can feel okay with you and your situation.

Ishana *shared these inspiring insights on solo motherhood.*

"I've always viewed being a single mum as a positive rather than something missing. It means we can up and go somewhere without having to check others' calendars. We enjoy precious one-to-one time, and are genuine friends as well as parent and child. Just being the two of us has meant we have met so many more lifetime friends than I think we would ever have done had we been a threesome or more, especially on holidays.

"It certainly makes you appreciate your support network and know that, whether you're a single mum or not, you're all just trying to do your best for your child, and maintain some kind of sanity at the same time. For me, making sure I exercise and see my amazing friends is my prescription, and so far it is working for both of us.

"Single parenthood is bloody hard work, but it's 100 per cent worth it, and I wouldn't change it for the world."

One of the things we love about Ishana's words is that they reinforce the idea that we can learn to love the experience of being a single-parent family – that there is nothing wrong with being a single-parent family, and it is still a *family*. Families come in all shapes and sizes, and what is most important is the connection between the people who love and are there for each other.

FINAL WORDS

As you journey through single motherhood, you will hopefully find the grief lifting and find ways to reduce the anxiety, the depression, the guilt, the worry. There may be a new flow to your life and your routine, from where you can reach for help and find *your* people.

You should start to notice you have more good days than heavy days, and that you begin to look up and forward toward the future, whatever that brings. You begin to find the time to know who you are, not as a partner or even as a mum, but just as you.

On your child-free days (if you have these) you begin to make choices about how you spend your time; you can discover what is important to you, what your likes and dislikes are, when you don't have to take anyone else into account.

You can start to create special traditions for you and your child, and treasure the times you have together.

You can think about new hobbies, new interests, new things *you* want to achieve. You can think about really, really looking after you.

We hope that you reach this place and find a way to feel like you are living your life for you. This isn't about putting on rose-tinted glasses – we know that single motherhood can be a tough, exhausting, emotional and, at times, frustrating, anxiety-provoking, rage-inducing overwhelmingly sad journey.

But we hope through this book and through these pages, despite all these challenges, you can find joy and hope and happiness, because you deserve it.

So, go out there and find it.

ACKNOWLEDGEMENTS

Dr Emma: I'd like to thank Amy Rose for her wonderful honest writing and being so generous in her collaboration on this book, and Beth Bishop for her ongoing guidance and support through this whole writing process.

As ever I am very grateful for my friends and family and my wonderful boys who have been endlessly supportive and patient as I have snuck in hours to write.

And most importantly a huge thank you to all the wonderful single parents who have made a difference to my life both professionally and personally, and to everyone who contributed their words and experiences for this book.

Amy: To all of the amazing single mums I got to speak to throughout this journey – thank you so much for trusting me to share your stories of solo motherhood.

I cannot thank Dr Emma enough for her incredible input to this book. Working with her has taught me so much and I couldn't have chosen a better person to collaborate with on this. Also, without the very patient Beth Bishop, this book would never have come to fruition! So, thank you so much, Beth, for trusting me and guiding me through this process.

Then, of course there's Milo – you're simply the best!

Lastly, thank you to all of my friends and family who never fail to have my back. I love you!

USEFUL RESOURCES

SINGLE PARENTING RESOURCES

UK
Child Maintenance: www.gov.uk/calculate-child-maintenance
Gingerbread: www.gingerbread.org.uk
MoneyHelper: www.moneyhelper.org.uk
One Parent Families Scotland: opfs.org.uk
Single Parent Action Network: singleparents.org.uk
Single Parents Support and Advice Services:
singleparentssupportandadviceservices.co.uk
Single With Kids: singlewithkids.co.uk
Turn2Us: turn2us.org.uk

USA
Family Lives: familylives.org.uk
Single Mother Guide: www.singlemotherguide.com
Single Mothers Grants: www.singlemothersgrants.org

AUSTRALIA AND NEW ZEALAND
Council of Single Mothers and their Children: csmc.org.au
NZ Single Parents: singleparents.co.nz
Single Mum: singlemum.com.au

APPS
Frolo
Headspace
Calm

MENTAL HEALTH RESOURCES

UK
Mental Health Foundation UK: www.mentalhealth.org.uk
Mind UK: www.mind.org.uk
Rethink Mental Illness: www.rethink.org
Samaritans: www.samaritans.org, helpline: 116 123
Scottish Association for Mental Health (SAMH): www.samh.org.uk
Shout: www.giveusashout.org, text 85258
Young Minds: www.youngminds.org.uk

EUROPE
Mental Health Europe: www.mhe-sme.org
Mental Health Ireland: www.mentalhealthireland.ie

USA
HelpGuide: www.helpguide.org
Mentalhealth.gov: www.mentalhealth.gov
Mental Health America: www.mhanational.org
National Alliance on Mental Illness (NAMI): www.nami.org
National Institute of Mental Health: www.nimh.nih.gov
Very Well Mind: www.verywellmind.com

CANADA
Canadian Mental Health Association: cmha.ca
Crisis Service Canada: www.ementalhealth.ca

AUSTRALIA AND NEW ZEALAND
Beyond Blue: www.beyondblue.org.au
Health Direct: www.healthdirect.gov.au
Mental Health Australia: mhaustralia.org
Mental Health Foundation of New Zealand:
www.mentalhealth.org.nz
SANE Australia: www.sane.org

SUPPORT FOR SUICIDAL THOUGHTS

If you are finding it difficult to cope or know someone who is, and need to be heard without judgment or pressure, you can find information and support from the following:

Crisis Text Line (US, Canada, Ireland, UK): www.crisistextline.org

UK
Campaign Against Living Miserably (CALM): www.thecalmzone.net
PAPYRUS (dedicated to the prevention of young suicide):
www.papyrus-uk.org
The Samaritans: www.samaritans.org

USA
American Foundation for Suicide Prevention: afsp.org
National Suicide Prevention Lifeline: suicidepreventionlifeline.org

CANADA
Canada Suicide Prevention Crisis Service:
www.crisisservicescanada.ca

AUSTRALIA AND NEW ZEALAND
Lifeline Australia: www.lifeline.org.au

DEPRESSION AND DIVERSITY

Black African and Asian Therapy Network: www.baatn.org.uk
Embrace Multicultural Mental Health:
www.embracementalhealth.org.au
The Institute for Muslim Mental Health
www.muslimmentalhealth.com/islam-mental-health

ABOUT US

Welbeck Balance publishes books dedicated to changing lives. Our mission is to deliver life-enhancing books to help improve your wellbeing so that you can live your life with greater clarity and meaning, wherever you are on life's journey. Our Trigger books are specifically devoted to opening up conversations about mental health and wellbeing.

Welbeck Balance and Trigger are part of the Welbeck Publishing Group – a globally recognized independent publisher based in London. Welbeck are renowned for our innovative ideas, production values and developing long-lasting content. Our books have been translated into over 30 languages in more than 60 countries around the world.

If you love books, then join the club and sign up to our newsletter for exclusive offers, extracts, author interviews and more information.

www.welbeckpublishing.com   www.triggerhub.org

🐦 welbeckpublish   🐦 Triggercalm
📷 welbeckpublish   📷 Triggercalm
📘 welbeckuk   📘 Triggercalm